Man of the Triple Name

JOHN B. KEANE

MAN OF THE TRIPLE NAME

BRANDON

To Kitty and Teddy

First published May 1984
Reprinted October 1987
Reprinted May 1990

Brandon Book Publishers Ltd
Dingle, Co. Kerry, Ireland

© *John B. Keane 1984*

ISBN 0 86322 061 4

Cover design: Paula Nolan and John Brady
Printed by The Guernsey Press Co. Ltd,
Guernsey, Channel Islands

Chapter 1

Dan Paddy Andy O'Sullivan, the last of the great Irish match-makers, was known from Portmagee to Tarbert and from Carrigkerry to the Cove of Cork. Outside this area he was no longer a household word but here and there would be people who would have heard of him. Whenever a man said he was a native of the Stacks Mountains, or more particularly Lyrea-crompane and Renagown, he was bound to be asked sooner or later if he knew Dan Paddy Andy O'Sullivan, the match-maker. While this brought pride and joy to most of the natives of the Stacks, others — a minority — regarded him in a poor light and I doubt if he was ever accorded the proper honour due to him. The nearer one came to his birthplace, in his heyday, the less likely one would be to hear his praises sung. Why this should be so is no mystery: a prophet is never recognised in his own land and Dan was often more outspoken than was good for him. By nature as well as by choice he unfailingly took the side of those without hope, position or property.

Still and for all he was probably the best-loved son of the Stacks Mountains even in his own lifetime, and his reputation has increased immeasurably since his death. In his later years television stations from all over the world sent their cameras to his door and there are memorable portraits recorded by the BBC, ITV, NBC and RTE, to mention but a few. (The great Alan Whicker paid a visit to Dan who endeavoured to make a match for him and, having failed, advised him to go to the famed resort of Ballybunion where, contrary to all opinions, Dan assured him he would meet up with a suitable virgin).

The last time Dan participated in a television programme was on the RTE series *Location* where he was an unqualified success and where he managed to milk more money from the producers than anyone else participating in the programme. He was, alas, forced to turn down subsequent offers because of ill-health. To the day of his death, however, he was engaged in the delicate art of matchmaking. When he was asked he could never fully explain why he chose such an odd vocation.

I doubt if I would ever have written a line about him but for a meeting with his son Jimmy while he was on holiday from the United States.

"'Twould be a great shame," Jimmy confided to me over a drink, "if his doings and sayings should go by the board."

It was this statement that bred my deep interest in the life and times of the greatest Irish matchmaker. I was lucky to know him personally and many's the time I brushed out his dancehall with him on Monday mornings after the night before.

I was hardly ten when I first visited Renagown, one of the more populous townlands of the Stacks, to stay with my relatives Martin and Jule Seán Sheehy in the house next to the famous Ivy Bridge. Dan's was the next house but one and we got on like a cow and a cock of hay from our first meeting.

I arrived from Listowel with a small suitcase towards the end of June in 1938 and I left for the first of many times at the beginning of the following September. I returned every year for those long summer holidays until, at the age of fourteen, I outgrew my boyhood and I stopped coming.

I still occasionally visit that friendly, secure home where I was half-reared, half-dragged up and countrified when Hitler was shrieking his head off in Berlin and innocent Irish men were dying in distant places like Tobruk and Alamein, men from the Stacks at that. Whenever I visit my friends and relations in that part of the world, Dan Paddy Andy's voice floats back to me and with it the faces of the old folk who have passed from the scene.

Approximately forty years before my arrival in the Stacks, Irish, as a spoken language, had taken its leave forever although there were still hundreds of words and scores of expressions in the everyday exchanges of the people. Jule Seán used Irish phrases regularly and could converse easily with Seán Kavanagh, a visiting Irish teacher from the Dingle Gaeltacht. Both she and Dan Paddy Andy remembered that Irish was spoken as widely as English by the old people when Dan and Jule were children. When strangers listened for the first time to English spoken in Renagown, they asked if it was Irish. The accent, it seemed, lived on but the language was dead.

It was here I met the characters who went into the making of my first play *Sive* and it was here I first heard the wonderful language — half-Irish, half-English — which Gabriel Fallon of the Abbey Theatre once asserted was spoken nowhere, but spoken it was in that time by man, woman and child in the Stacks Mountains. Of late it is losing its colour and the Gaelic phrases are dropping by the wayside but the language is still unique and has an undercurrent of pure poetry.

No portrait of Dan Paddy Andy O'Sullivan is possible without a brief introduction to the Stacks Mountains where he spent his life. It is against the background of this largely untrodden hill country and against the lifestyles of its people that his status must be measured. From here he plied his trade. When his family and friends left he remained behind. He was too integral a part of the scene to ever consider emigrating and in the end he died where he wanted to die, resigned and serene among his few remaining friends and neighbours.

Chapter 2

The North Kerry Stacks differ from all other mountain ranges in many ways. Principally, I daresay, it is because their inhabitants do not regard them as mountains at all and indeed it must truthfully be said that whoever it was ascribed to them the majestic name of mountains in the first place was more of a hyperbolist than a cartographer.

"Stacks Mounds would be more like it," quipped a journalist friend. The truth is that the Stacks are too high to be hills and too low to be mountains, therefore I feel we should give them the benefit of the doubt and grant them the lofty designation of mountains.

They contain only two summits in excess of 1,000 feet. These are Beenageeha at 1,062 feet and the more southerly Ballincollig which stands at 1,170 feet. Nearly every townland is inhabited, which is more than can be said for most ranges. The Stacks resemble a triangle in shape with each angle situated approximately four miles from the towns of Listowel, Castleisland and Tralee. To the east of the Stacks stand the Glanrudderies, really an extension of the Stacks and locally regarded as part of the Stacks.

The best known townlands in the Stacks proper are Lyreacrompane, the most famous, and Renagown, birthplace of Dan Paddy Andy O'Sullivan. In the latter, most precious, most sacred and most streamful of spots, the storied Ivy Bridge spans the Glaishe Riabhach along whose leafy banks I made my first fumbling attempts at writing.

Some other well known townlands in the Stacks are Muingnaminnane and Broughane. The stream known as the Glaishe Riabhach, after tripping its way across Renagown, links up at Lyreacrompane proper with the main river of the Stacks which is the Smearla. This in turn joins the Feale River at Inchamagillery about three miles from Listowel which town it half encircles with a life-giving embrace before proceeding at a leisurely pace to Ballybunion of the champagne air, early spuds and short-lived summer romances.

That part of the Glanrudderies nearest to the Stacks is

known as Knight's Mountain. Around this area is to be found the friendly village of Knocknagoshel, well frequented in his heyday by Dan Paddy Andy and famous for the slogan "Arise Knocknagoshel and take your place among the nations of the earth". This was boldly painted across the banner borne by the Knocknagoshel Parnellites when they marched to Abbeyfeale to welcome their uncrowned king, Charles Stewart Parnell. Well known townlands in the vicinity include Knockanebrack, Cloughboola, Knockaderreen, Muingwee, Fahaduv and Glashnanoon.

There are other places with equally fanciful and beautiful names and these shall also arise and take their places among the nations of the earth before we draw to a close. English translations of many of these place names may be found in Paddy Lysaght's excellent publication *Notes Towards a Short History of Duagh*, published by The Treaty Press of Limerick.

When I first went to the Stacks, my relatives and, equally so, my parents in Listowel were doubtful about the capacity of a young townie to endure a period of more than two months away from the bustle of town but they need not have worried. I fell immediately in love with this strange and wonderful countryside, with the character, colour and language of its people and with its numerous dancing streams from the sensitive Glaishe Riabhach to the dashing Smearla.

The unbounded freedom of hills and glens amounted to sheer paradise. Every day I would disappear for hours and become part of that vast and lovely countryside. The Stacks have a magic all of their own. Where the green pastures and meadows merge into the boglands the dominating colour is brown, but it is a changing brown that is a mixture of every brown, and all are subject to the whimsy of the hill winds that alternately fill and empty the skies of the shadow-making clouds. At worst the brown is sober, at best burnished gold, but ever and always it is a brown that is warm and comforting.

Chapter 3

I came to the Ivy Bridge in a creamery lorry driven by Tim Canty of Listowel and I left in a fishcart driven by an agent of the Listowel fishmonger Jumpin' O'Hanlon. I forget who the guide was on that occasion but I'll never forget Jumpin' O'Hanlon who owned a successful fish shop a few doors down the street from my parents' house in Listowel.

Jumpin's agents would come to Renagown throughout the year, but in September the great man himself might accompany the cart which would be piled high with crate upon crate of fresh mackerel. He would come by the Six Crosses, Tournageehy, Pike, Rathea, Lyre Cross and Carrigcannon to the Ivy Bridge and the Cross of Renagown, stopping at chosen spots along the way to dispose of the plump, mouth-watering mackerel, always at their finest in September and early October. Jumpin' came to be seen and he came to be heard. His full name, of course, was James Jumpin' Alive O'Hanlon. He acquired his unusual soubriquet from the way he responded when asked by Dan Paddy Andy if his mackerel were fresh.

"Dan dear," he would say, "they're jumpin' alive."

Jumpin' was always received at the Cross of Renagown by Dan Paddy Andy himself and his wife Kitty.

"Are they fresh, O'Hanlon?" Dan would open the ritual and Jumpin' would provide the traditional answer. Then for the benefit of everybody present Jumpin' would seize an outstanding specimen and hold it between his hands in such a way that it seemed to jump from his grasp of its own accord.

"Stop that fish; stop that fish somebody," he would call. "Stop it in God's name, don't it go home to Cahirciveen."

That would be the commotion as we went on all fours to seize the mackerel which, as soon as it was recovered, would jump out of his hands again until finally he was obliged to rap it on the head with his knuckles to make sure it didn't return to that wild part of the Atlantic from whence it came.

Dan Paddy Andy was never a man to indulge in loud laughter. If anything he was a chuckler, but he was unable to restrain himself when Jumpin' O'Hanlon arrived at the Cross of Renagown. There were other itinerant fishmongers who made the long journeys from Castleisland and Tralee but none had the charm or cajolery of the great O'Hanlon save perhaps one Tommeen Mountain whose true name was Thomas Prendeville. He used a well-worn Baby-Ford to transport himself and his fish.

In the Stacks (Knocknagoshel apart) there were no villages, but there were several shops. I recall Lyreacrompane Post Office, Doran's, Nolan's and McElligott's, where I was dispatched every Wednesday to bring home the week's supply of home-cured butter, and beautiful butter it was. In Tralee and Listowel it was called farmer's butter. Then there was Dan Paddy Andy's famous dance hall of Renagown Cross where lemonade and biscuits were often available on Sunday nights. As well as the fishmongers, there were several itinerant butchers and an occasional travelling salesman. These were mostly Pakistani with huge suitcases of wispy undergarments, scarves and frocks perched precariously on the carriers of rickety bicycles. I remember two of these. There was "Likey Nicey Tie" and "Likey Nicey Knickeys". The latter often indicated that he would be prepared to exchange his wares for female favours. As far as I know he never did any business in this fashion although there was a strong story circulating in Tralee that he was once seen staggering into that songful town clutching the saddle of his cycle for support and not as much as would outfit a leprechaun left in his outsize suitcases.

In our youthful ignorance we would stalk these unfortunate pedlars as far as the Cross of Renagown shouting, "Likey Nicey Tie, Likey Nicey Knickeys," and most heinous of all, "Likey Piecey Pig's Bum". We had been informed by a local hobside theologian that our coloured brothers would be automatically damned if they consumed any form of pig meat but doubly damned if the portion came from the pig's behind. The only excuse I can offer for these unforgiveable discourtesies is that we didn't know any better.

Then there were the travelling insurance agents who called every week for sums ranging from a sixpenny piece to a half-crown. Those insured were generally old people and when they expired the money went to meet funeral expenses. These included advertising in the newspapers, the cost of high mass, a decent suit or habit for the corpse, a coffin and a pound note each for low mass to priests outside the parish who might attend the funeral. Then there were black coats, black dresses and black ties for the next of kin, black muslin to make armbands for relations near and distant and 10s. for the parish clerk. Finally, there was the wherewithal to purchase a sufficiency of porter, whiskey, wine, minerals, barmbracks, ham, jam, shop bread, snuff, tobacco and what have you to be given according to their tastes to all those who came to mourn.

Few households could afford such expense and it was common practise to insure rather than suffer the disgrace of a threadbare wake or, worse still, no wake at all. The insurance men were well-dressed and courteous and were never without low shoes, locally called slippers, as well as collars and ties, Sunday suits and, for distinction, a row of fountain pens and pencils adorning the top pocket of the coat. The more fountain pens, the more established the agent. They came mostly on bicycles and small motor-cycles and a chosen few possessed Baby-Fords.

Every townland was possessed of a least one pig butcher and the better-off houses had an array of salt flitches hanging from the ceiling for all to see. They used to say at the time in Renagown that a man was indeed well provided for who had a pig on the ceiling, a pig in the barrel and a pig fattening.

Bacon and cabbage or bacon and turnips always boiled together for flavour and served with boiled potatoes invariably made up the main meal which was served at noon and referred to as "the dinner".

Calves, heifers, bullocks and cows were dispatched regularly to the fairs of Listowel, Tralee and Castleisland but fresh beef was a rarity in most households of the Stacks.

In this country the milch cow was queen. She provided milk, cream and butter and in most farms, big or small, the monthly creamery cheque was the only source of income. Even the humblest of landless hovels boasted its own cow. Roadside grazing was abundant throughout most of the year so that little winter fodder was needed.

Chapter 4

The time when I first became acquainted with Dan Paddy Andy was a period of considerable hardship for Dan and for most of the population of the Stacks although they bore their lots with good humour. The great turf deposits of Lyreacrompane and Renagown were yet to be exploited. Money was scarce and so was employment but there was a certain degree of self-sufficiency. Farmers and cottiers alike grew enough potatoes and vegetables to feed themselves and the equally deprived population of nearby towns. The problem was to find money for luxuries like flour, tea and sugar. There was a limited demand for turf but the price hardly made it worthwhile. The going rate was 2s. per assrail, 3s. 6d. per pony rail and 5s. per horse rail — and for this the rails should be clamped high and the quality good. A high-clamped horse rail of black turf could weigh as much as a ton. When the supply exceeded demand in the market places of the surrounding towns, the rails were knocked down at rock bottom prices and it was not uncommon to see an assrail of turf changing hands for as little as 1s. 6d., but even this paltry sum was sufficient to purchase a week's supply of tea and sugar for an average family, say five children and two or three adults.

Other luxuries such as butter and jam were not easy to come by whereas the 2d. for the paper packet of five Woodbines was even more difficult to acquire.

In those naive days it was the consensus of opinion that while smoking retarded growth in adolescents it did no harm to adults and was often looked upon as a sort of panacea for nervous disorders. This was particularly true of pipe smoking in the countryside and an old man or old woman without a pipe was something of a rarity.

Bendigo Plug was the most popular brand of tobacco and every shop counter sported a thick leather covering over an area a little less than a foot square for the sole purpose of cutting the Bendigo from the giant coil into which it was compressed. There was also a special cutting implement or tobacco knife, in appearance much like a miniature hayknife.

Hundreds emigrated to America, Canada and Australia but the vast majority boarded the boat for England where the native manpower was wholly expended in the struggle against the Axis. The only positions open to the labour forces of the Stacks Mountains were those of serving girl and farmer's boy until the escalation of the war brought the import of English coal to a trickle and for the first time the peat bogs of the Stacks Mountains came into their own.

That was the best time to be in the Stacks. While the demand for turf lasted there was no man or boy who didn't have a shilling in his pocket. Man, woman and child took to the bogs across the spring and summer and for the first time in the history of the area every household had a pound or two to spare.

The turf buyers would come from Listowel, Tralee, Castleisland and Abbeyfeale to estimate the size and quality of roadside ricks which would fill the wagons waiting at the railway depots in the aforementioned towns. Those who journeyed to the depots with horse, ass, mule and pony rails clamped high with the heaviest sods were met a mile or more outside the urban boundaries by gratuitous buyers.

In addition the Kerry County Council, for an all too brief period, initiated a turf-cutting campaign in order to supply cheap fuel to the many institutions under its care. The Council rates in 1943 were 5s. 10d. per day for under-eighteens and 8s. 4d. a day for over. This was a generous wage for the period. It was a boom time in the bogs but, alas, shortlived.

This then was the stage for Dan Paddy Andy's activities. From his modest home in Renagown he fared far afield in the furtherance of his calling. His farm, which carried eight milch cows, a work-horse and a smaller number of dry stock, for a while barely provided for himself and his family's needs but he was never a man to submit to hardship and so we see him endeavouring by every stratagem at his command to improve their lot.

Chapter 5

No picture of Dan Paddy Andy would be complete without a glimpse into that early time when matchmaking was the furthest thought from his head and when his chief concerns were the filling of his stomach and keeping himself reasonably well clothed and decently shod.

His schooling was scanty although in later years he was to blossom into an outstanding scholar, fully acquainted with the lore and history of the Stacks Mountains and armed with a thorough knowledge of the people who dwelt there. This localised insight and understanding was, as far as Dan and his matchmaking were concerned, what education was really all about.

"The road is the best college," Dan once confided to Tom Doran as they sat in front of the hearth one night planning the musical programme for the dance of the following Sunday night, "and the road is the best teacher to shape a character and I promise you, Tomáisín, I have plenty of the road behind me."

In Dan's boyhood there were only two kinds of scholars, the very good and the rest. The very good were those who topped their classes and went on to be teachers, civil servants, road stewards and auxiliary postmen in that order.

Few, if any, of the major professions emerged from this countryside in Dan's youth. In those days a pupil might remain on at the National School if he so wished until he reached the age of sixteen, but there were few parents who could keep on feeding a non-contributory adolescent up to this point.

Anyway if a youngster remained on until this advanced stage and failed to acquire one of the aforementioned positions he would always be treated with extreme suspicion by local employers, the vast majority of whom were farmers.

This suspicion arose from two factors. Firstly it was regarded as a fait accompli that a youth who spent so much time in the classroom was rarely fitted for manual work on a farm. Secondly it was widely accepted that an educated agricultural labourer would be fonder of agitating than working and that the quicker he was shipped off to America or Australia the better for the entire agricultural system of the Stacks Mountains.

The perversity of all this as local farmers saw it was that these scholarly dodgers were quite capable of consuming as much food and demanding as much money as those who worked themselves to the bone.

A substantial farmer who lived not far from Dan and who had the misfortune to employ a number of these enlightened slackers over a period of years once suggested at the height of a sustained drinking session in Al Roche's pub that the only way of dealing with them was to shoot one in every four as a warning to other malingerers of the same ilk.

Apparently they had contaminated other less enlightened labourers with mutinous talk of shorter hours for more money, annual holidays and equality at mealtimes — i.e., the right to sit at the same table as their employers and a guarantee of the same type food.

As well as this they managed to fertilise the more innocent serving girls in their districts before departing the scene for all time.

On the other hand dunces and fools made excellent drudges. They never questioned because they did not know how to question. All that concerned them was a bed, a smoke, three square meals in the round of a day and an occasional drinking bout. They evinced little interest in the opposite sex for the good reason that they were so exhausted by the end of the day they were fit for nothing but bed.

Educated workers made impossible demands for the time that was in it. Consequently nobody wanted them. Most of them succeeded beyond their wildest dreams in America, Australia, Canada and England and flaunted large, flashy automobiles over the dirt roads of the Stacks to the mystification and envy of their former employers whenever they arrived home on holidays.

There is absolutely no doubt but that they nearly all did well in the countries of their adoption. When they boarded the emigrant ships they took their dignity and their education with them. English was the spoken language of their new abodes and during a time when emigration was a way of life in the poorer European countries a man with fluent English who could read and write without difficulty had a headstart over less fortunate exiles who had no English at all.

While Dan Paddy Andy was not a great scholar neither was he a dullard. He fell somewhere between the two stools. His sight, which always troubled him, turned him into a slow learner. Consequently he had little difficulty getting work from a farmer. At fourteen he was a well-built fellow, destined in time to take over his father's farm. His younger brother Din Paddy Andy would later become a member of the Garda Síochána, serving for the best part of his career in the city of Limerick before retiring to Killarney where his widow still lives.

A year after he left school it was decided that Dan should go into service with a farmer. The year was 1914. The First World War had been precipitated by the murder in Sarajevo on 28 June of Archduke Francis Ferdinand, heir to the Austrian throne. Austria then declared war against Serbia, and Russia prepared to tackle Austria. Germany declared war on Russia and then set about invading France and Belgium. Britain declared war on Germany. Japan, rather than be left out of it, declared war on Germany. Russia invaded Austria and Germany. Britain declared war on Turkey. This was war fever on an unprecedented scale. Never before in the history of mankind was there such an eruption of bellicose hysteria.

In Renagown, heartland of the Stacks Mountains, however, things were calmer, although the district was invaded one sunny Sunday afternoon by a red-faced wobbly-bellied East Limerick farmer by the name of O'Leary.

When word went out that young Dan Paddy Andy was available for agricultural work there were few immediate offers. It was already late in the year with the fall beckoning. It looked as if it might be the following February when the annual hiring of farm labour took place before he could expect to be employed fulltime.

O'Leary arrived in a horse trap and explained that the boy who normally worked for him had disappeared without trace. "The poor fool has probably gone off to fight in the war," O'Leary explained. At O'Leary's request Dan was brought before him and inspected from head to toe. Assuring himself that Dan was sound in wind and limb O'Leary put him through his paces. Dan was reasonably well versed in the use of a shovel, spade, pike, slasher and scythe and was a proficient milker. O'Leary owned 120 acres of prime pastureland which maintained forty milch cows.

"There's myself and the wife," O'Leary told Dan's father and mother, "and we have a fine hardy girl, so the work will be fairly divided and there won't be any great strain on your gorsoon."

He would require Dan's services until the end of November. A bargain was eventually struck after O'Leary agreed to certain conditions. What he didn't disclose was that he hadn't a sop of hay cut and that he had twelve acres of corn ripening.

Dan put on a brave countenance as he said goodbye to his mother. So it was with the impression of his father's hand hard on his and with the early July sun high in the sky that Dan Paddy Andy O'Sullivan left home for the first time.

He was to say afterwards that O'Leary was the making of him, "because," said Dan, "if a man isn't apprenticed to hardship when he's young he'll make no fist of it when he's old."

After a non-stop journey of six hours they arrived at O'Leary's abode. Straightaway, with the help of O'Leary's wife and an old crone who hastened from an outhouse to untackle the horse, they turned into the cows. The fine, hardy girl, it transpired, was none other than the crone.

"She could have been a sister to the Hag of Beara," Dan recalled. "She was that ancient."

The hours went by while Dan Paddy Andy weakened with the hunger. As the light began to fail they finished the milking but there was still no word of food. Dan decided to make his feelings known.

"Sir," said he to O'Leary, "I didn't put a bite inside me since the noon of the day."

O'Leary acted as if he didn't hear him aright, for all he intimated to Dan was that he would be well advised to make straight for his bed since they would be rising with the sun in the morning.

"Sir," said Dan in a louder tone which O'Leary could not fail to hear, "I'm starving with the hunger."

O'Leary looked at him for a full minute before speaking.

"You only think you're hungry," he said. "Your sleep will be destroyed by nightmares if you put food in your belly this late hour of the night."

"I don't care," said Dan. "I must have something to eat and I must have it now."

It was a long time before O'Leary spoke. Before he did he laid a paternal hand on Dan's shoulder and then came the most contrary caution ever heard by the youthful Dan Paddy Andy O'Sullivan up until this time.

"If you listen," said O'Leary, "I'll give you some sound advice."

"What advice would that be?" Dan asked.

"It's a foolish youth," said O'Leary, "that puts food in an empty stomach at night time."

Dan was so genuinely confused by this that he went to bed in a daze without a bite of any kind. The following day just before noon he told O'Leary that he had no intention of starving to death.

"I was always used to enough," said Dan boldly, "so if things don't improve I'll write to my father."

"You may be sure," said O'Leary, "that the grub here from now on will put such a blossom and a shine on you that your father and mother will be wondering who the fine stranger is when you return to them in November. But neither do we want to send you home like a fat pig. My advice to you is eat enough but never more than enough. Always keep one thought before you and you'll do well in the sight of God and man. Always remember that gluttony is one of the seven deadly sins."

The day in question was Friday, a day of fast and abstinence at the time.

"If I had been at home in Renagown then," Dan told me later, "I'd be facing for my fine fried mackerel or a pair of herrings; and if there was no fish there would be the finest of onion sauce with new spuds and butter and a panny of buttermilk to wash the whole lot down. If what I've re-counted wasn't on the menu there would be three or four fried eggs and spuds galore or maybe a slab of well-steeped ling in its own dip with a knob of butter in the middle."

In the kitchen of the O'Leary farmhouse there were two tables: the main one for the farmer and his wife and two

19

young children, the other — a smaller rickety one — for Dan and the old crone.

"She was so old," said Dan, "that she forgot where she came from. She worked for her keep and the occasional half quarter of tobacco. She spared her pension money for to cover the costs of her funeral which wasn't long at all after that. She never spoke, only grunted. May the good God grant the creature a silver bed in heaven. She was nothing but a slave."

There were many like her at the time. Rather than abide in the workhouses they preferred to slave until the day they died for thankless employers. There was a stigma, totally unjustified, hanging over the workhouses of the time and later over the county homes. These institutions were spotlessly clean, the food was plain but plentiful and there was no scarcity of tobacco. In those days the vast majority of elderly women smoked dudeens, i.e. shortened clay pipes which could be concealed in the fist if strangers called or daughters-in-law disapproved.

When Dan and the old woman sat down to the meal at O'Leary's, the farmer's wife went up into the Room and returned with a five foot high screen which she placed between her own table and that of the servants. This was so that Dan and the crone could not see what was on the main table and to discourage any high-faluting notions they might entertain with regard to food. Finally, after she had served her husband with his meal, she attended to the wants of Dan and the old woman.

She placed a plate on the servant's table with several old and wizened spuds on it, explaining that the new ones weren't fit to be dug just yet.

This was a lie because Dan had seen O'Leary pulling stalks earlier in the morning. After the spuds came a small jug of skimmed milk and one lone, middling-sized bawnie or white hen-egg. At home in Renagown no one would eat a white hen-egg. Eggs had to be speckled or brown or even off-white. White hen-eggs were given to calves and greyhounds but never to humans. There was the same lack of regard for white calves. On the other hand there was no objection to white women according to Dan.

"Blasht me," said Dan, "but there was fierce demand for

white skin on women and little or no demand for yellow or brown skin when I was a gorsoon and what matter but one was no better than the other inside in the bed or out of it."

"Is there any more eggs coming up Missus?" Dan enquired of the farmer's wife.

"Wisha what do ye want more for," said she, "haven't ye a heap of spuds and plenty milk. Divide the egg now like a good boy and 'twill keep ye going handsome till the supper."

"Here," said Dan, pushing the egg under the old woman's nose, "let you carve."

On some weekdays and on Sundays there would be meat, either fresh or salted, but there was never enough of it and it was always fat. There was only one vegetable and that was kale.

"I was coming to believe," said Dan, "that there was no more lean meat left in the world, so I put it to O'Leary that I would have to get a fair entitlement of lean meat. However, he gave me such an account of the effects it had on the human stomach that I wasn't sure whether fat or lean was the best.

"Many's the time my thoughts went back to my mother's flahool table in Renagown. Any man passing the road might turn in there and be sure of a hearty welcome plus the fill of his craw. Since that time I never saw the bate of O'Leary and I met many a strange character during the course of my travels.

"I left O'Leary the end of November. I saw him once only since then and that was at Listowel Races after the war. He was eating a penny bun and I swear to you the same man could buy out half of Listowel. A man without a heart is no man and you may be sure that neither O'Leary nor his wife ever died from heart attacks because they had no hearts. I left O'Leary," Dan went on, "with welts and callouses all over me, with a stoop on my back that stayed for six months and with a loss of a stone and a half in weight. But it was a profitable experience. It made me appreciate the decent home of my father and mother and I never complained again when goodies were scarce or if there was no shilling in my pocket. I must say though, in all fairity, that O'Leary and his wife were well-matched. I couldn't have made better myself. You may be certain of one thing," Dan said sagely, "and that is this. If O'Leary's children don't drink his hard-earned monies you may be sure that his grandchildren will because that's the way of the world and 'twas a wise man said that the scatterer comes after the gatherer."

This was to be the last time Dan would work for a farmer. When he inherited the farm at Renagown he set to work at once draining and fencing it. When he applied himself to farming he had few equals but the simple truth was that his interests lay elsewhere. He believed that it was more profitable to work the head.

Chapter 6

When I first met Dan Paddy Andy it must be said that his name was already a household word in Listowel, the town of my upbringing. Almost every home in North Kerry had a different story to tell about the last of the great Irish matchmakers. Some of these were not too complimentary, while others were far-fetched and even outrageous.

I had only been in residence a week or so at Renagown when Dan landed to the Sheehy household and demanded an interview with me. How Dan became aware of my presence was beyond me at the time. I was as mystified as my relations by this unexpected request but, to make a long story short, I was speedily located and ushered into the formidable presence of this legendary figure. Although it was a warm summer's day he wore a black frieze overcoat with the shaggy nap more pronounced than usual and a hat with an unusually broad rim which cast a shadow over his face. He also carried a stout blackthorn stick and wore a pair of spectacles with lenses as thick as plate glass. Somebody once compared them to the bottoms of two empty jampots. There was no doubt but that Dan until his declining years could see a good deal through these uncommon eye pieces but I doubt if anybody could see in.

A schoolgirl who was once asked by the reverend mother of the Presentation Convent where she was a pupil to interview Dan Paddy Andy said of him, "Dan Paddy Andy was a medium-sized man with broad shoulders, a sallow complexion and a stubborn jaw. He had a lilt to his voice that would charm the birds off the trees and a courtliness in the presence of women which exceeded that of all the other males in the Barony of Iraghticonnor."

He shook hands gently and accepted the offer of a sugawn chair from the man of the house Martin Sheehy while Jule Seán, the woman of the house, arranged a ring of glowing coals at the side of the hearth next to the fire. The kettle was already on the boil.

The smaller of the two earthenware teapots in everyday

service was removed from the dresser and first rinsed with boiling water before the tea leaves for the tea proper were added to the pot. Only then was the teapot filled and the tea allowed to draw on the bed of coals. No table had been set nor was there any intention of sitting at table for this was not regarded as a major meal. It was known simply as a "cup out of the hand", an in-between refreshment where the visitor was handed a cup full of tea already coloured and sugared and without the aid of spoon or saucer.

If Dan had been a visitor with a long journey behind him the table would have been set with the best the house had to offer and the larger teapot pressed into service to indicate that there was no limit to the number of cups the visitor might drink. In the Stacks Mountains and in Renagown in particular, during my boyhood, visitors were never asked if they would care for tea or food. Always the woman of the house would silently see to the kettle and lay the table to suit the occasion. It would be unheard-of not to prepare refreshments of some kind the moment a visitor put his or her leg inside the door. The best in the house was never too good for even the lowliest caller. Nothing was ever expected in return. It was all part of the code of the Stacks.

Dan Paddy Andy accepted his cup of tea and loudly voiced his gratitude by expressing the fond wish that the household might never want for the bite and sup.

There followed the customary rustic preamble before he got down to cases. This concerned itself with weather, crops, births, deaths and marriages and when it ended there was serious speculation about the international scene. The burning question of the time was how long the Finns could hold out against the Russians and I well recall that after the evening Rosary at Sheehys of Renagown there were additional prayers for the welfare of the Finns up until the time peace was declared between Russia and Finland in March of 1939.

Local characters who bore some resemblance to European leaders and dignitaries of the period were called after them. There was Smuts, Petain, Sir Stafford Cripps (an elderly pensioner), Rommel, Franco (two elderly batchelor brothers) and what have you.

When all topics of international interest had been exhausted

Dan Paddy Andy announced that he had been notified by his friend Pat Kenny, the Church Street victualler in Listowel, that I was sojourning with my relations in Renagown, that I had a collection of coins and consequently might be some sort of authority in the advanced science of numismatics.

My collection was small and practically worthless and my knowledge smaller still but the latter I placed unreservedly at the disposal of Dan Paddy Andy who had over the years amassed a large collection of coins at the door of his cross-roads dancehall.

These had been fraudulently substituted for legitimate coin of the realm. Dan Paddy Andy's sight was so poor that his only means of testing a coin was to bite it with the few sound teeth which the passage of years had left in his head or to feel it with his fingers although these must have been rendered somewhat insensitive from years of attachment to slean, shovel and pike, not to mention the paps of cows and the rock-hard sods of Lyreacrompane turf which he had handled since childhood.

The biting system was admirably suited to the discovery of pewter, tin and leaden coins but it was a complete failure otherwise. Dan's collection was as varied as it was interesting. It consisted chiefly of well-worn farthings with beautifully grooved edges and flattened out a little so that they resembled English sixpenny pieces when blanched with silver paint or covered with fine silver paper which was to be found in most cigarette boxes of the period. Next there were halfpennies blanched as well to resemble shillings and neatly grooved. Then there were dimes and nickels which Dan was not above accepting when Irish coins were not available.

Threepence was the then rate of entry into the dancehall. In a separate small bag there was a collection of fake English threepenny pieces. These numbered 500 and had been punched out of a sheet of tin by an army corporal who sold them at a penny a time. Irish troops were under canvas in Renagown for most of World War II, but more of that later. Months were to pass before Dan Paddy Andy discovered that he was being taken in by these tin pieces. In time Dan acquired a taste for copper and silver and would often suck the dubious lucre as though the pieces were lozenges. If he was satisfied that he was being duped he would spit out the counterfeit coins in disgust.

There was a large number of religious medals, the chief of which was a sawn-off Child of Mary medal, originally oval in shape and which now resembled a florin. It was perfectly grooved and it was the one piece in the entire collection which annoyed Dan Paddy Andy every time he looked at it. What niggled him was the fact that he had given out 1s. 9d. change upon receiving it.

"If I could catch the hoor who committed that sacrilege," said Dan, "I'd have him excommunicated."

Chapter 7

My most vivid impression of Dan Paddy Andy is etched indelibly in the memory. We were all seated at the supper table in Jule Seán's one fine evening in the early summertime. The year might have been 1938 and then again it might have been 1939. God be with the times. We were eating yellow meal pointers, McElligott's butter and boiled eggs as I recall when Dan's considerable shadow cast itself across the doorway.

"Don't no one stir," was his first salute. His second was to bless all present and his third was to bless the work in hand.

"I can see," said Dan as he surveyed us one and all, "that there is no iochtar in this litter." He refused the offer of supper.

"I only stopped in for a second," said he, "to take the weight off my feet." He was handed a chair which he placed near the doorway. He sat where he could avail himself of the failing daylight. He leaned forward on the sugawn, his mighty hands resting on the knob of his ashplant, his hat down over his forehead, his hobnailed boots planted well apart as his spectacled eyes feebly sought the outlines of the hills beyond the doorway.

"How goes the matchmaking, Dan?" Martin Sheehy asked.

"Hither and over like a cow's tail," said Dan and we all laughed. As the light failed his outline darkened in the doorway. Only a Goya could have thrown together the nuances of light and half-light to capture Dan Paddy Andy as he was then. For a moment he took off his hat to scratch his poll and in so doing he threw back his great head and gave forth with a long and loud yawn which reminded me of an old and tired lion readying himself to settle down for the night.

His voice was rich, mellifluous and engaging and he spoke as if he knew the exact value of every word. He never uttered a commonplace observation. In the neighbouring towns of Castleisland, Listowel and Tralee his accent might be described as tuathalach but those who ascribed this description to it were unwittingly paying him a compliment.

As we scooped out our eggs and wolfed back the pointers Dan settled himself in his chair and proceeded to tell us about the first match he ever made. This historic event began in the town of Castleisland in 1935 during the morning of the last turkey market before Christmas.

Dan left home early that morning in the company of his wife. His transport was pony and rail. His cargo consisted of eleven turkeys, four prime cocks and seven plump hens. Castleisland has one of the widest main streets in Ireland, the second widest in fact, and it was here the turkey market took place. The Lyreacrompane turkeys had a good reputation. Dan's wife, in particular, had a good name for rearing only the best. The hens were always serviced by the best cocks available and if this necessitated a long journey to a certified station cock then a long journey was made and the cost of the cock's service was never reckoned. Dan, of course, had no time for turkeys. He had a preference for roast or boiled goose and no blame to him, for it was widely held in the Stacks that the soup of the latter would bring a body from the brink of the grave. Turkeys, however, greatly added to the income of the small farmers in the Stacks and there were few that did not rear and fatten a clutch for the Yuletide.

In no time at all the Renagown turkeys were sold and with the proceeds from the sale Dan's wife took herself off to buy the Christmas. Meanwhile Dan was left with two hens. These had been purchased by a spinster from the nearby vale of Cordal, famous for football and moonlighters. Hence the song:

> Ye brave boys of Cordal, ye made a brave stand
> Ye worked night and day to keep Walsh on his land.

One of the conditions of the sale was that Dan would pluck the hens for the Cordal woman for, as she explained to Dan, she couldn't pluck a wren. As Dan neared the end of the plucking she arrived on the scene. She was a small, wiry lady, according to Dan, with a gait of going like a water hen and a tongue that lent itself to non-stop chatter. Yet she was a decent sort of damsel. She never questioned the price of the birds having satisfied herself that the quality was there. She lived with two sisters in a one-storied, thatched farmhouse. None of the three were what we might call fledglings but they were honest, God-fearing and no strangers to hard work.

When Dan finished he handed over the birds with the announcement that they were as bare of feathers as babies' bottoms. The Cordal woman gave him a shilling tip, no mean sum in those days.

"'Tis a wonder, Miss," said Dan, "you wouldn't make out a man of your own to pluck those turkeys for you?"

"Yerra," said she, "where would I get a man, me that goes nowhere except to mass and market."

"Faith," said Dan, "if you have a mind for a man I mightn't be long making one out for you."

"Go 'long with you," said the Cordal woman. "Who would be bothered with the likes of me?"

"Leave it to me," said Dan, "and keep your thoughts to yourself."

All the time Dan had been searching his mind until eventually he came upon a suitable partner. We shall call him Hourigan.

"Do you know Hourigan, the travelling fishmonger?" Dan asked her.

"He's well known to me," said the Cordal woman.

"What do you make of him?" Dan asked.

"I have no fault to find with him," she said. "I always found his mackerel fresh and his herrings wholesome."

"Go about your business now," Dan instructed her, "and please God you won't be taking a hot water jar to bed with you next Christmas."

Dan sent out word through the market that he wanted to see Hourigan. Time passed and in the heel of the evening Hourigan landed, leading a pony and cart on which several boxes of fresh herrings were displayed.

"How many do you want?" Hourigan asked.

"I don't want any," said Dan.

"They're supposed to be great for the brains," said Hourigan.

"I'm sure there's no fishmonger would gainsay you on that score," answered Dan, "and anyway," said Dan, who was cleaning out his car after the turkeys at the time, "I have brains enough for the job I'm at just now."

With that he tethered his pony to Hourigan's and invited him for a drink. In the pub Dan Paddy Andy held forth about the happiness of marriage and the suitability of the Cordal woman. Hourigan was a lonely fellow of middle-age without chick or child who realised that time was running out on him.

Between the jigs and the reels the wedding took place before the following Shrove. The pair were happy and content and Dan was paid a £10 note for his trouble with a proviso that another £5 would be paid if there were male issue or 50s. if the issue were female.

Dan had often been involved in the making of matches before this to pass away the time, as indeed had most people in the Stacks Mountains. The important thing about the Castleisland pairing, however, was that the initiative was taken by Dan and Dan alone and, most important of all, he received a fee for his services for the first time ever. He resolved as a result to become a fulltime matchmaker.

Generally speaking judgement was suspended to see how the relationship between the Cordal woman and the fishmonger would work out. It would be a good test of Dan's sense of compatability.

Hourigan was a quiet, hard-working fellow, well-liked, a decent man in a pub and a good worker, but how would he work out in sole charge of a woman? Would he blackguard her when the early bloom of their relationship began to fade? Would he, a confirmed batchelor, conform to home life and keep regular hours?

Then what about the Cordal woman? Long in the tooth wasn't she and capable of talking the hind leg off a pot! Would she be able to cope with a character as rough and ready as Hourigan? There was much speculation as to how the marriage would be faring, say after the first year.

Women from the Cordal side reported, after this space of time, that Mrs Hourigan was as happy as a woman could wish to be and that while Hourigan was without polish or posh manners he was always kind to his wife. From all reports and appearances a great and lasting contentment seemed to be building up between the two.

So Dan's name was made. After the success of the Hourigan tie-up, men and women would come from every corner of Kerry to seek his aid. Later they would come from as far afield as Cork and Limerick and occasionally, on fine Sundays during the summer, there would be the odd visitor from Clare, Galway or Tipperary.

He always maintained that it was that first match between the fishmonger and the Cordal woman that started him off on the road to success.

"If that arrangement had gone astray," he confided, "I might not have made a trade of the thing at all, but when I saw the happiness and comfort I brought to Hourigan and his woman I knew that the Man Above was anxious for me to pursue with my efforts and to make life aisy for them that was in danger of being left to one side."

Chapter 8

Over the twenty-five years during which Dan Paddy Andy actively plied his trade of matchmaking, he was responsible for over 400 marriages and of all these only one was a failure. Whenever he reminisced over his colourful career this particular disappointment never failed to surface. He would shake his head regretfully and blame himself for what happened.

The reality is that he was in no way to blame. The failure was due to the fact that the female partner of this unfortunate liaison was incapable of any sort of sexual confederacy because of excessive religious commitment and belief in the variety of taboos which would seem to suggest that even marital sex was a shameful business. She was, consequently, unwilling or unable to play her part in that area of marital obligations so carnally and unpoetically referred to as the consummation.

The marriage, therefore, was a fiasco, and of her own accord the bride returned in due course to her own corner of the hearth in her father's house where she lived unhappily ever after. The first husband brought in another woman in the course of time. He referred to her as his housekeeper and who are we to say that she was anything else. They had a son a priest and a daughter a nun and you don't have progeny like these where you have irreverence and impiety.

Hard to blame the poor woman since it was a time when even the mention of sex brought instant condemnation. Visiting missioners thundered and railed against sins of the flesh almost to the total exclusion of all other transgressions.

In the pulpit and indeed the confessional an unhealthy and unnatural attitude to sex was often fostered. Single girls in particular were subjected to the most insensitive and inquisitorial of interrogations in confession. Those who transgressed were frequently obliged to name the partner and to give a detailed description of every aspect of the act of copulation. Those who did not transgress too far were asked to define the nature of kisses, if these kisses were mere affectionate pecks or if they were long, lingering or passionate.

Some priests seemed obsessed with the sexual behaviour of the penitents. Could it be that they were subconsciously trying to impose on others the same celibate strictures to which they themselves were subject or was it that total sexual deprivation had frustrated and tormented them to such a degree that they behaved the way they did? Maybe excessive religious zeal was the root cause.

Then there were the missioners who were not above rounding up local mass and confession drop-outs and herding them willy-nilly to the mission devotions and, of course, salvation. The missioners would go so far as to invite the congregation to secretly submit the names of impious neighbours and acquaintances so that they might be prayed for and visited by one of the missioners who would point out to them the error of their ways and entreat them to return to the bosom of the church.

What made England doubly attractive at the time was that as well as being assured of well-paid jobs the emigrants, for better or for worse, found themselves in a land where free-love was, more or less, taken for granted.

In the Stacks Mountains there were at least two curates armed with flashlamps and stout sticks who spent their nights chasing courting couples. One of these priests had a pedigreed terrier called Rex, a veritable bloodhound for sniffing out courting couples who, when discovered, would run for their lives with the terrier yelping at their heels and the priest loudly enunciating forecasts of eternal damnation as he vainly endeavoured to keep pace with his hysterical canine.

Many of these couples would have been wending their romantic ways homeward from Dan Paddy Andy's tiny dancehall at the Cross of Renagown. Consequently Dan came in for frequent condemnation from numerous pulpits contiguous to his stamping ground. Then there was the story of the lost slippers, a sort of paradigm-in-reverse of the Cinderella fable. It happened towards the end of the war in 1945 around the time Berlin capitulated to the Russians and ironically around the time when rural Ireland had almost capitulated to the compelling influences of many of the clergy.

The story of the slippers is still recounted in the Stacks whenever the wartime period is recalled. The incident happened near Castleisland. A courting couple happened to be roving hand in hand one night through a moonlit bohareen, addressing themselves no doubt now and then to the stars and whispering to each other those sweet little nothings which are the heart and soul of innocent courtship, although according to many of the clergy of the time courtship was anything but innocent. Then, suddenly, shortly after the midnight bell tolled from the nearby town the dreaded ecclesiastical footsteps were heard in the distance. The couple's worst fears were realised when the investigative sniffing of the curate's terrier drew nearer and nearer to the small sally grove where they had hidden themselves at the sound of the first footfall.

Inexorably the dog closed in and as soon as he had pinpointed his quarry the frenzied yelping began. Panic stricken, the young sweethearts ran off in different directions ignoring the curate's ultimatums to give themselves up. Alas, in her flight, the girl lost her slippers but she did manage to get away safely without being identified.

The following day the curate called to every farmhouse and labourer's cot in the district and asked the householders if they had ever seen the slippers before.

"Why, yes," said one ingenue when the curate visited one of the last of the farmhouses in the suspect area. "I declare to God if they're not Pegeen's. Thanks very much, Father."

The admission very nearly drove the owner of the slippers to distraction. Fortunately her parents knew her for the virtuous girl that she was and the curate was sent about his business.

We see, however, the sort of benighted opposition with which Dan Paddy Andy had to contend while trying to keep his dancehall open.

It is difficult now to understand the rôle of many of the local clergy during the Thirties, Forties and Fifties. Their main aim seemed to be the oppression of country people or, at least, those country people who were genuinely terrified of the Roman collar.

While Dan's dancehall activities were regularly condemned by less tolerant members of the clergy there was no criticism of his dealings in matchmaking from that influential quarter. No doubt the church recognised the dire need for made marriages in isolated places where the tradition was late marriage and often no marriage at all. It followed as night follows day that if there were no marriages there would be no christenings. Nobody who was familiar with Dan's activities of the time recalls a single onslaught from the clergy because of the matchmaking. Tom Doran sums it up.

"He brought the priests extra business year after year," said Tom, "and they wanted that business badly. You'd think on that account they'd say nothing about the bit of dancing as a favour to Dan."

It was once rumoured at the creamery of Lyreacrompane that two men wearing black suits and white collars called to Dan in the dead of the night in the summer of 1943. They summoned him out of his bed and gained access to the house by giving the impression that they had lost their way. Inside they ordered Dan to go on his knees and to renounce his ways. They asked him to give a sworn undertaking that he would never again open his dancehall during the Lenten period.

According to neighbours, Dan, who was immensely strong, knocked their heads together and chased them as far as the Cross of Renagown from where they made off in the direction of Glounamucmae. Some said the pair were from an order of Brothers while others insisted they were priests from a not-too-distant parish. Others claimed they were a pair of well-known blackguards from a nearby town. No information was ever forthcoming from Dan about this incident. The pair should have known better for Dan Paddy Andy's knuckles were like iron and his grip was the grip of the badger, no release till a bone was heard to crack. He never courted trouble in his life, however, and although he was often challenged by be-grudgers who looked askance at the business of matchmaking he never reacted unless he was positively forced to defend himself.

Although opposition of the clergy finally forced the closure of his first dancehall at Fahaduv, Dan Paddy Andy's second at the Cross of Renagown survived their strictures until it closed due to different, secular reasons.

Dan was always most reticient when questioned about the priests who closed his first dancehall and tried hard to close the second.

"Only a priest has the right to chastise," Dan would say.

"Dan Paddy Andy has no white collar and so Dan has no right to chastise."

Regularly in his later years newspaper reporters and television interviewers would endeavour to draw him about the Catholic Church. Always he stoutly refused to be drawn. Quite often, in fact, priests sought out his services for friends and relations and many priests on holiday from America and England who hailed from the Stacks orginally would take him out for a night just for the crack. He was great company and while the local men and women would often be tongue-tied or at least cautious in the presence of the clergy Dan had no such inhibitions.

"The suit may be black," Dan once said of a holidaying priest who was a bit of a character, "and the collar may be white but you can't expect the blood to be anything but red. Those that do are hard on priests."

There was one period in Dan's life when several priests in the parishes affected by the Renagown dancehall took it upon themselves to make a concerted attack on the flouting of diocesan laws regarding Lenten dancing. The Lenten ban was observed by the proprietor of every dancehall in the diocese of Kerry with the notable exception of Dan. He found himself very much alone during this period with only a handful of bogadawns and hardchaws attending the hall on Sunday nights. Even some of his friends deserted him during this period. Kate O'Brien, his wife, was also affected but she was never a woman to interfere. There is absolutely no doubt that any other man in similar circumstances would have cracked under the pressure. Dan took the whole business in his stride knowing that it must inevitably blow over.

Quite a number of parents, during this period, forbade their offspring to cross the threshold of the Renagown hall. For a while it seemed certain that it would go the way of the Fahaduv hall and the hall at Kilflynn Cross but Dan persevered even though it meant running the hall at a loss. Then magically the attention of the priests was diverted to another and a much more ancient form of transgression. There began a wild and unfounded rumour that wives were being swapped wholesale in a certain golf club not too far away. This is a recurring rumour in the small towns of Ireland and one which presents a great outlet to mischievous and over-imaginative men and women. It gives them the chance to add on their own agusheens to the prevailing slanders. After the disappearance of the gentry and the great houses it was obvious that a new source of improbable sexual activities would have to be found if the imagination of the common people was not to be stifled. The local golf club was the logical successor. It attracted the professional people and the leading business people.

Nobody wanted to hear stories about ordinary people. Only in recent times have most clubs lowered their qualifying standards for membership so that nowadays most clubs accept anybody possessed of the membership fee.

Luckily for Dan the rumour escalated and he was left off the hook. If it wasn't a wife-swapping scare it would have been something else such as a new crop of loose women in some nearby town or a strange tale of buggery.

So the Renagown hall had a reprieve and after a short period the old patrons drifted back until business was normal once more.

Chapter 9

Another phenomenon of the times was the Behan Line in Ballybunion. At the time the Siegfried and Maginot Lines of Germany and France were central topics of discussion with World War II looming.

In 1937 Fr William (Billy) Behan succeeded Canon Michael Fuller as parish priest of Ballybunion and in so doing inherited one of Canon Fuller's pet aversions. This was the prevalence of mixed bathing against which Canon Fuller had unsuccessfully pulpiteered for years. There have been many controversies concerning the goings on in Ballybunion during its summer seasons but none excited more interest than the Behan Line.

Before coming to Ballybunion, Fr Behan had built a name for himself as a man who got things done. He had successfully renovated the parish church of Ballyheigue when such a venture was considered to be an act of folly because of the prevailing poverty of the times. The parish of Ballyheigue which he had vacated in favour of Ballybunion and of which he had been parish priest had a reputation as an impeccable family resort. This may have been due in part to the fact that it was avoided by those in search of sinful pleasure.

However, there can be no doubt that Fr Behan, a truly godly man, was a powerful influence, as well as being a tireless agitator against immorality; although there were many who would be quick to tell you that he carried out most of his crusading where no immorality existed at the time. However, it cannot be denied that he would have been possessed of inside knowledge because of his calling and would have been infinitely more familiar with dubious activities within his parish than any hurler on the ditch.

After his arrival in Ballybunion he bided his time but with the advent of the first summer season he recognised that the resort had special problems. In spite of several sermons advising against and eventually proscribing mixed bathing, he was horrified to see that there was an increase rather than a decrease in what he saw as an occasion of temptation.

Ever the man of action he tried a novel tactic. He chose a certain spot on the Men's Strand and charted his plan of campaign. There were, by the way, and still are in Ballybunion two beaches: one known as the Men's Strand and the other known as the Women's Strand. Fr Billy caused a line of wooden stakes to be driven deep into the sandy floor of the Men's Strand and made it known that the area between the stakes and the rocky, cliff face of the Castle Green promontory was ever afterwards to be a sanctuary for bathers of the male species many of whom would have been priests. On the other hand all males were excluded from the female area.

It worked. Even the fathers of families forsook their wives and children and although for many it may have been for one of the resorts, excellent public houses or hotels, the majority contented themselves in their own restricted area. If, from time to time, some luckless female or females accidentally strayed on to the male domain there were cries of outrage from both sides of the divide.

For several years the barrier existed but eventually attitudes began to soften and more adventurous females occupied stretches of the restricted beach in increasing numbers. By the time the first bikinis appeared there was no sign of Fr Behan's paling sticks. Today if you ask any one of the young lovelies who frequent the Men's Strand when and where was the Behan Line, I'll lay a pound to a penny there's not one will tell you.

Fr Behan lived to the ripe old age of ninety-one and is fondly remembered in the lovely resort where he once reigned supreme. This then, give or take an exception, was the religious climate of the period and this was the background against which Dan Paddy Andy flourished against all the odds.

Chapter 10

In this chapter I would like to recall a strange, and indeed wonderful, incident which I hope will provide the reader with a fuller insight into the complex character who was Dan Paddy Andy. I think it will show that he was equipped to cope with any sort of emergency but more especially that when disaster seemed imminent Dan showed that he had the flair and the special humour to turn the tables on misfortune.

I would like, therefore, to write about the band that wasn't there at all. The events leading up to this strange phenomenon occurred in 1936 which was the year of the closing down of the dancehall at Fahaduv Cross which lies between Lyrea-crompane and Castleisland. A lot of other things happened in 1936. Edward VIII became King of England but abdicated before the year was out. Germany was rumbling and grumbling. The writing was on the wall when the Rhineland was occupied. Abyssinia was conquered and annexed by Italy. The Spanish Civil War broke out in July and did not end until March of 1939. Then there was the collapse of the League of Nations. It was shown to be without teeth. Hitler and Mussolini came together under the Rome-Berlin Axis. There was the Anti-Comintern Act between Japan and Germany. In short, the seeds of world war were being sown in various parts of the world. Around the same time the parish priest of Castleisland declared war upon Fahaduv dancehall. The broadsides were purely verbal.

The hall was the forerunner of the famous hall which Dan Paddy Andy was to build shortly afterwards at the crossroads of his native Renagown.

Here is what the venerable Archdeacon Browne, parish priest of Castleisland, had to say from the pulpit to a breathless congregation one Sunday morning after Dan opened the Fahaduv hall:

"I now have something to say about a nearby den of iniquity and it is high time it was said. There is a wild animal after descending from the mountains on Fahaduv and it is the man of the triple name, Dan Paddy Andy." In a lengthy sermon the archdeacon told his flock to shun the new dance-hall.

At the time Dan was "rabbit-shooting" at the back of the church. In those days, rabbit-shooting was the name given to the posture of male massgoers who refused to take a seat in the body of the church, preferring to kneel on one knee with an elbow cocked and resting on the other upraised knee. Immediately after the archdeacon's outburst Dan arose and addressed the other rabbit-shooters in his immediate vicinity.

"There's no mark on me," said Dan, "and there's no scar after that man's spake. He don't know but I do that God won't be hard on Dan." Then Dan tiptoed from the church and went off to the Fahaduv hall for the afternoon dance.

For a while after this Dan was looked upon as a pariah. He cared little. What mattered was that the Fahaduv dancehall did excellent business, although only for a while, as a result of the archdeacon's proscription. It was the best and the cheapest publicity that any of Dan's enterprises was ever to receive. More than one crossroads dancehall had been closed by priestly intervention in North Kerry during the benighted decades before and during Word War II.

Not long after the Renagown hall was opened Dan engaged a local national teacher to write to Lord Haw-Haw requesting him to give the hall a plug in one of his many sarcastic commentaries from Radio Bremen. Haw-Haw never obliged and never acknowledged the letter although he did make reference to the town of Rathkeale in county Limerick less than thirty miles from the borders of Renagown. In that reference Haw-Haw claimed that the British army wouldn't beat the tinkers out of Rathkeale on a fair day. Whatever about that Dan Canty of Renagown assures us that Dan Paddy Andy O'Sullivan single-handed and handicapped by failing sight beat a large band of blockers out of Castleisland horse fair after an altercation about a horse.

"He struck no man a second time," said Dan Canty. "He didn't have to. One lick from Dan and you stayed down."

Fahaduv was a small hall with a corrugated iron roof. Its capacity was 200 people. Admission was 2d. on weeknights and on Sunday afternoon, rising to 3d. on Sunday night. This charge was further increased to 4d. if there was strange music, i.e., any sort of music outside the locality but especially musicians from neighbouring towns. Nearly always, however, in both the Fahaduv and Renagown halls a single accordeon or melodeon player supplied the music from start to finish.

When the Fahaduv hall was closed towards the end of 1936 Dan transported the roof to cover the new hall at Renagown. It was the clergy who closed down Fahaduv. Not a trace of the building is to be seen at this present time. The clergy felt justified and many God-fearing people might agree. Dan insisted on holding dances there on all nights during the Lenten period and on Christmas night as well. At the time there was a diocesan ruling that there was to be no dancing of any kind during the periods mentioned although in certain neighbouring dioceses there was no ban except on occasions such as Good Friday night and Christmas night. Dan ignored the Kerry ban and left the parish priest of Castleisland with no option other than to instruct his flock to stay away from the hall at Fahaduv. The majority of the patrons who abided by the clergy's ruling would be parishioners for the most part. In the end the publicity attracted too many undesirable replacements.

But what about the band that wasn't there at all?

It happened that on the fateful last night in 1936 a townie band was billed to play at the Pallodium which was the name Dan gave to the Fahaduv hall. On the night in question the Pallodium was packed to capacity but no band showed up. It transpired later that the band leader was struck on the face the night before by a baby's bottle which his wife flung at him when he arrived home drunk with lipstick on his collar. His nose was broken as a result.

The other members of the band, a saxophonist and a drummer, had gone off without notice to fight on opposing sides in the Spanish Civil War. Towards ten o'clock the crowd began to grow noisy and there were shouts of "money back!" Several fights broke out, although according to Dan these consisted mostly of mauling and shouting and there was never any danger of a riot.

"In all my years of dancehalls," Dan was later able to boast, "I never sent for a Civic Guard or I never called on any man to back me up. It was my hall and I made sure everyone knew about it."

Certain that the band would come sooner or later Dan

Paddy Andy went on the Fahaduv stage and provided some lively puss music until relief should arrive. He was a good didler and in no time at all the quarter sets were in full swing. He knew he could not hold out all night but suddenly assistance came from an unexpected quarter. According to Dan, who was running out of breath at this stage, he was joined on the bandstand (eight wooden planks atop four tar barrells full of stones) by a man wearing a zipped gansey and a secondhand Civic Guard's trousers. This man immediately sat on one of the three chairs which had been provided for the absent musicians. He then pulled out one of his galluses from under his gansey and with a long cipín or stick, which he happened to have in his hand, proceeded to simulate a fiddle player. From the side of his mouth came a sound which resembled fiddle music. Dan looked closely at him during the first interval and recognised him for a half-fool who had spent a good number of years "behind". "Behind" was the name give to the mental home in Killarney. Dan decided not to interfere. The crowd seemed to enjoy the poor fellow.

When Dan resumed his didling the music, supplemented by the fiddling, was much improved. Better still the dancers were growing less restive. Then without warning another man jumped on the bandstand of the Pallodium. In his hand he had a newspaper which he had folded into the shape of a trumpet. He took a chair and started to play.

"No hound, nor no cat," Dan Paddy Andy told me later, "no chimney wind, nor no banshee could howl like this man." Whatever about this claim it seems he greatly augmented the fiddle music. It took Dan a long time to recognise him.

"He was a chap of the neuter gender," said Dan, "from the Raemore side but m'anam ón diabhal he could supply music and music of any kind was never so badly wanted. He lost his contraption, the poor aingisheoir," Dan continued "when a chairoplane gave under him one night at Listowel Races but a happier nor a more contented poor creature you never could see."

Shortly afterwards the band was joined by another member. This newcomer was a schoolmaster who was undergoing a fortnight-long booze after the death of his mother.

He took over as conductor of the band. He was followed by a gorsoon who brought with him an empty biscuit tin and two laths from the back of a chair.

"I declare to God," said Dan Paddy Andy, "but he was a born drummer. We had a full orchestra in right earnest and the crowd went wild as the night wore on. Fair play to the musicians, they never took their eyes off their conductor and whenever he asked for extra he got it. When he asked for it soft he got it soft and when he asked for it loud he got it loud. The sweat ran down the faces of the musicians. Their shirts were stuck to their backs. The dancers bawled and roared and you couldn't ask for better diversion."

The dance, according to Dan, went on till cockcrow, at which precise time the musicians collapsed. Dan roused them briefly while the conductor stood like a ramrod, his hands held high, ready to declare the first note of the National Anthem. This the band played with great fervour and devotion while the crowd stood stock still. Not a soul moved till the anthem was played out to the finish.

Dan Canty was present on that crazy occasion.

"I never saw anything like it," said Dan. "Sober men went wild and women that never raised their voices before went screechin' like snipes around the hall. It was pure bedlam. Everyone was afflicted. People just wore themselves out. There will never be a night like it again. It was once in a lifetime." The following Sunday, Archdeacon Browne made reference to the mass hysteria and human degradation but he was misinformed. Said a clerical student of the time, now himself a parish priest: "I honestly believe it was the best thing that could happen in that it changed all those who were present for the better. My own brother said it was the most hilarious night he ever spent in his life and he still recalls it as the most outstanding experience of the era."

The night had a specially beneficial effect on the afflicted. The teacher ended his alcoholic shaughraun and went back to his school. The fool was no longer a fool or, as Dan said, "It would seem he was no longer a fool." The night released whatever it was that kept him for so long in a backward state. The drummer later became a professional drummer and ended up with his own band. The chap who played the trumpet made of newspaper learned how to play the saxophone and although nothing could be done for his ailment he had little time to think about it so much was he in demand on festive occasions.

Dan himself was greatly relieved. The dancers enjoyed themselves so much that it never occured to them to ask for their money back. In fact many were later to say that they never laughed so much. Man, woman and child in the Stacks Mountains laid claims ever afterward to having been present but only 200 souls were lucky enough to hear the band that never came.

There was only one sour note. Two of the musicians, the so-called fiddle player and the drummer, came to Dan's abode at Renagown the following night and demanded payment for their contribution of the night before.

"Show me yeer union cards," said Dan, "and ye'll be paid in full."

The drummer explained that they had no such cards.

"In that case," said Dan, "there can be no talk of payment for if I was to pay either one of ye I could be transported under the act. However," Dan continued, "I am not a mean man nor would I like it to go out about me that I was mean. So what I'll do now is this. I will leave two single shillings here on the window sill and go back to my warm hearth. If by chance the two shillings should vanish who is to say what happened." So saying Dan placed the two coins on the window sill and withdrew.

Shortly after the Pallodium was closed forever. The walls stood firm for a while against the onslaught of wind and rain. Today there is no trace of the Fahaduv hall but there is a publican's wife in Tralee who simply collapses with mirth whenever "the night of the no band" is mentioned.

Dan Paddy Andy, however, never took anything lying down. Having abandoned the Pallodium he immediately set up business in Renagown. There was, however, no more dancing on Sunday afternoons. That was the only concession he would make to the clergy. Towards the end of his days he was on excellent terms with nearly every priest in the district but while the dancehall flourished he was destined to be at loggerheads with "the clan of the round collar," as he nearly always referred to them. Yet Dan was a devout Catholic who never deliberately missed mass. His wife and children were equally devout and are still affectionately remembered all over the Stacks Mountains. Dan himself put down the antagonism of the clergy to jealousy.

"They can't fill the parochial halls," said Dan, "whilst I have no bother filling my hall. In law they can't close me down and they can't turn me into a goat either."

Dan also held card gambles for geese, bonhams, cartons of cigarettes and even donkeys. The game played was forty-one. Around midnight before the playing of the finals the players would march down the road to Jule Seán's where tea and bread and butter or bread and jam was provided. Jule Seán Sheehy of the Ivy Bridge always had a great regard for Dan Paddy Andy and generally encouraged his numerous enterprises in any way she could. Dan made a modest profit from the card gambles but even this innocent amusement drew dishonourable mention from certain pulpits on the grounds that the participants stayed up all night and were unable to work in the morning. Anyway, at that time card-gaming was regarded in the same light as unseasonal dancing by many of the clergy.

Chapter 11

The Renagown dancehall of Dan Paddy Andy O'Sullivan was under severe pressure from all sides from the day it was built. However, the first of the death blows was not struck until the foundation was dug for a relatively large dancehall at Headley's Bridge on the Dublin to Killarney road, halfway between Abbeyfeale and Castleisland. The name given to this new edifice was simply Headley's Bridge hall. This once popular venue has also been closed for several years now, gone the way of the Pallodium, the Renagown hall and Dan Connie's loft, gone the way of many a crossroads dancefloor and roadside platform. Slowly but surely as Ireland emerged from the Frightful Fifties the economic situation began to improve. This improvement was painfully gradual but it built up year after year until the end of the Sixties when it blossomed into full flower. Gone was the memory of the Economic War, a conflict incidentally in which only a country like Ireland with its incredibly exotic forms of ultranationalism dare indulge.

Motor cars became plentiful and on Sunday nights boys and girls were forsaking the village and parochial halls and venturing further afield to the bigger towns and even to the cities.

One by one the old halls, many of them tiny, capable of accommodating no more than a hundred couples, disappeared. They had, however, played an important rôle in the life of the countryside when there was no transport only the occasional bicycle or the pony and trap.

It could be said that Dan did more for his own people during the Thirties and Forties than any other man of his time. Paddy Kavanagh, the poet, would have appreciated Dan. He might have written a poem to him had they met or had he known about his activities. Dan stood like a rock against anything and everything which might stifle the right of people to enjoy themselves, the right to kiss and pay court, to love, to marry, to dance and to sing their way out of the dark ages of the Economic War.

While many of the younger priests and many of the itinerant missioners of the time would sympathise with Dan they dare not air their opinions in public. Many priests were bitterly opposed to Dan but we should remember that when times are black for the ordinary people they are blacker still for their priests and before we hasten to condemn the more outspoken and ancient of these rude clerics we must not forget that they were only carrying out orders and were ill-prepared for frontline duties when dire family emergencies arose. Looking back it could be argued that most of the strictures of those impoverished times were necessary if human dignity was to be preserved. Dignity does not thrive where there is poverty. At best it survives. The danger arises when strictures, religious or otherwise, become intolerable. Human dignity will be the first thing to take a knock.

Priestly interference caused the closure of a crossroads dancehall between Tralee and Listowel during the heyday of the Renagown Hall. Until recently the ruins were visible from the roadway but now nothing remains. The miracle is that Dan Paddy Andy's Renagown dancehall survived for so long in the face of such opposition.

Without doubt a number of priests who should have known better went out of their ways to ruin Dan Paddy Andy and yet most people who knew him will remember him as the one pure spring in the stagnant waters that were the Thirties and Forties.

No matter how deformed or distorted one's body or features one need never despair while Dan was around. He was the arch-enemy of loneliness and whatever faults he may have had his compassion was boundless. A large proportion of his matches were engineered without any hope of monetary reward but simply out of the goodness of his heart.

"There was nowhere to go and nothing to do until Dan became an impressario," Tom Doran recalls.

The Renagown hall was somewhere to go and a place outside of which older people could congregate on fine nights for the want of something better to do. There was no television. Radios were still a luxury and would remain so until long after the end of the war. On the credit side there was a good deal of bothántóireacht or rambling and there were many established "rambling houses" where a lonely man was made welcome and given a place by the fire. Women rambled much less and if a woman lived alone or was looking after an aged parent it was unlikely that she would have the courage to face up to the door of a rambling house although her welcome would be assured. Still for the most part women did not ramble.

For younger people rambling was not the answer. Young men and women longed for the sight and touch of each other. Winter nights were lonely and although the homes were happy with card games and stories you could not fulfil a dream of young love from the corner of a kitchen table. You cannot keep a young man from thinking of girls no more than you can stop the sap from quickening in the brambles of spring.

No man knew this better than Dan Paddy Andy and I often suspect he needed the hall at Renagown as much as its rustic patrons did. His lifestyle shows that while he was happily married to Kate O'Brien there was also a hunger in him for life and excitement as well as travel. He never waited for things to happen. There was need for a hall at Renagown so he went and built it. There was need for a matchmaker in the Stacks Mountains so he made matchmaking his profession.

Dan Paddy Andy was ever up and doing. The dancehalls he built at Fahaduv and Renagown, little more than sheds really, were as much for his own edification and amusement as for the rustic patrons who came flocking there and who had, until Dan's enterprise surfaced, been completely at sea in the more sophisticated ballrooms of Listowel, Abbeyfeale, Tralee and Castleisland. He was a popular man but he was not without enemies. His success as a matchmaker and as a dancehall proprietor left him better off than most and there were many who envied him but according to part-time taxi driver Dan Canty, Dan Paddy Andy simply could not hold on to money. He was no great lover of intoxicating drink although he was fond of a session with his cronies or with the interested parties at the conclusion of a successful bout of matchmaking.

The hall is now but a memory but on one occasion Dan aided the clergy when he made a memorable speech after it was brought to his attention that certain ladies from the surrounding towns were misbehaving after leaving the hall.

"It has come to my attention," said Dan, "that townie pullets are laying out. If their wings get clipped me nor mine will not be accountable, and I say to these doxies that they can steer clear of here from now on."

Dan also frowned on young gentlemen who stamped on the floor during reels and sets. Low shoes were worn by few and strong boots, often hobnailed, were the order of the day. Consequently there was a printed notice tacked conspicuously on to the wall immediately inside the door. All it said was: "No pounding". Admission was 4d., strange music (town music or musicians) 6d. and for this you could dance from dusk till break of day.

There was one particular tune popular during the war that was anathema to Dan. This was "Horsey, horsey, don't you stop". According to Tom Doran, who with his accordeon was the resident orchestra in the Renagown hall for many years, the opening bars of this tune were the signal for deafening pounding on the already shaky floorboards. The minute Dan heard the tune, he called a halt to the music and climbed on to a stool.

"If you have that much taspy for horsey-horsey," said he, "ye can have it on the way home."

"Horsey-horsey" was, in fact, responsible for a minor calamity which occured around 1943. There was a capacity crowd in the hall and as there was no likelihood of more customers Dan paid a brief visit to his nearby house for a cup of tea. On his way back he heard the pounding. The anger surged up within him, for remember the large notice which stated explicitly that there was to be "No pounding".

The floor of the hall was upraised and consisted of thin wooden slats nailed to wooden joists. When Dan arrived part of the floor had collapsed. The first thing he did was to stop the music. When the music stopped so did the dancers, all save two bogadawns and their women. A bogadawn was the name given locally to big, soft, backward farmers' boys who were obliged to return to the National School to receive religious instruction for a belated Confirmation.

Bogadawns of the time were notoriously wayward. Dan was, therefore, obliged to knock their heads together as was his wont when dealing with those who flouted his rules. This stopped their bucklepping quickly enough. Dan went on stage immediately and made one of his famous announcements:

"Let it be known," said he, "that there is to be no more of this thing called 'Horsey-horsey'. Anyone I catch at it will be barred from this hall for life and, moreover, I will leave his rear end in such a state that he won't sit down for three months."

The following day he hired a carpenter to repair the floor. He also put up a second notice inside the door. It read simply: "No Horsey-horsey." He took it down after a fortnight lest the nick-name stick to him.

Chapter 12

I remember when I was on holiday at the Ivy Bridge, young farmers' boys on bicycles would make incredibly long journeys just to have a look at Dan Paddy Andy. Often they went home well pleased with themselves having only seen the notorious hall at the Cross of Renagown. Families would come in horse and pony traps for a glimpse of the great man. When Dan was in the humour he might condescend to talk with the visitors, but business was business and he reserved his more gifted powers of conversation for prospective clients.

Often a troupe of bachelors of mixed ages, for the want of something better to do, would put aside a feast day or Sunday for a visit to Dan but these were merely looking for estimations of their own worth. Often too a strong farmer would arrived with a backward bachelor brother, relative or neighbour with no notion of entering into serious negotiations.

"Out for a day's sport," said Dan, "but if you were to turn up a raving beauty for one of these bucks, an only daughter now, with land and money in plenty, they might oblige you by marrying her."

However, the real bane of Dan's life was visits from rogue bachelors who merely wanted the names and addresses of single women who might be induced into an intimate relationship with no prospect of marriage.

"Some prime bucks used come to me from Tralee and Listowel and there was a jockey from Abbeyfeale, but I soon settled that sort of thing by reporting them hoors to the Civic Guards."

It transpired that the visitor from Abbeyfeale wasn't a jockey at all. Rather was he a foppish fellow who was fond of wearing plus fours. It is a remarkable but true fact that all those mischievous suitors who tried to degrade Dan Paddy Andy's vocation suffered serious ill-luck sooner or later.

Dan once told Tom Doran that for every genuine client there would be at least three bogus ones.

"I got so's I'd know the genuine ones in the course of

time," he confided. "You see, Tomáisín, there's a haunted look in the eye of a man that's on the last legs for a woman. They does be dribbling from the mouth in desperation."

Towards the end of his career Dan was approached by a widow who had been happily married for many years to an active and powerful man. She scorned the advances of lesser men after his demise and she once declared to Dan Paddy Andy that she was now dependent on the electric blanket for heat, comfort and consolation.

"I have a mighty man for you," Dan said, "from the townland of Scartaglin and 'tis an electric fence you'd want to keep him from consoling you."

The man promised by Dan Paddy Andy turned out to be all that Dan said he was and another happy partnership was added to the great matchmaker's impressive list of successes.

While Dan might admire men like Pope John 23rd and Rudyard Kipling, he most assuredly would not hold with certain of their more memorable pronouncements. Pope John repeatedly warned against the dangers arising from too much ostentation and we have Kipling saying in his oft-quoted poem "If", "That we should not look too good nor talk too wise." On the other hand Dan would subscribe fully to the views of Polonius on this topic. Did not he say, "Costly thy raiment as thy purse can buy."

Dan Paddy Andy was completely in favour of display and he would advise his clients to doll themselves up and scrub themselves spotlessly clean in readiness for the first meeting with a prospective bride or groom.

"Remember," said Dan, "that some of my clients were awkward fostooks without manners of any kind, as coarse as sandpaper and wild as colts. I often see them myself and they firing cadhrawns at girls in order to attract their attention. Some of those same cadhrawns would be heavy and hard and would you blame a poor girl if she ran away instead of turning around. There were some of the girls and they were no better. Snapping the cap off a fellow's head was considered great sport entirely. Off she'd run with the cap in the hope that the owner would give chase. This was often what I had to play with. Is it any wonder the aingisheoirs couldn't fend for themselves in the marriage stakes."

What Dan said was true of many bachelors of the time.

They were often so unruly that one would be forgiven for thinking them mad.

"I was often asked," said Dan, "how I would go about judging a man or a woman. The first thing is to remember 'tis not an ass nor a cow you're dealing with and I would say that money should be of no account although I hate to admit, it was the big thing in all my dealings. Still if money is there it shouldn't be thrown on the fire. The best of men and women started with nothing but what God gave them; and this is the most important of all, to be thankful that the good God shaped you in a natural way for the world. Every time I look around me and see an unfortunate person with a mawcal I thank God and I ask myself why was I so lucky. I'm sure that those with mawcals must be asking why they were so unlucky that done wrong to no one. Size or shape or weight should make no difference in a man and a person that goes by these alone is in for troubled times as sure as there are stars in the roof of the sky. Look at the size of Napoleon and wasn't he the hardest root of all times. Wasn't Queen Victoria only a dumpling and didn't she reign the longest of them all.

"For a man to be too decent is not good either. A decent man is only a nickname for a fool. The best man is the man that puts his family before all. That man will have peace of mind and the grace of God."

Dan was often fond of boasting that there was no man or woman he couldn't marry if he put his mind to it and provided it wasn't improper.

"M'anam ón diabhal," he would say to Martin Sheehy of Renagown, "if you can train an ass to conduct himself, shouldn't it be easier train a man?"

Many of Dan's clients were men and women in their late forties and early fifties. Many suffered from nervous disorders and depression for want of contact with their fellow human beings. Through inability to make contact they isolated themselves more and more until finally they found themselves living in quiet desperation with nowhere to turn. Dan sought out these people of his own accord. He had seen too many end up in the mental home in Killarney. In those days there were no neighbourhood clinics or visiting psychiatric nurses. As a consequence the mental home was filled. Many of its occupants should never have been sent

54

there but there was no other option at the time.

Dan's intervention came as a great blessing to these unfortunate people. I remember once in the holiday house in Renagown to hear Jule Seán say to Dan, "It's a wonder you don't get a woman for Morrisheen So and So. He's turning into himself and starting to act queerly." Dan never turned a deaf ear to such a plea. His critics should remember that in steering these people on the road to a normal life he was performing a social service of immense magnitude. At the time there was no person or no institution capable of providing such a service. Dan was well aware that loneliness was part and parcel of everybody's make-up and for those who were mentally unable to adjust themselves to confront it, the only solution was a partner.

Approaching these sensitive people required great tact and compassion and if there was no money following such labours Dan always maintained he was well rewarded when such people settled down successfully. If he never did more than seek out these recluses he would have been an important figure in the community. As always many so-called respectable people felt that the unfortunates aided by Dan had no right to marry at all. Dan would often be told, "Leave them alone; aren't they fine the way they are?"

The trouble was that they only seemed fine the way they were and sooner or later without Dan's intervention the inevitable would happen.

Chapter 13

For many years Dr Johnny Walsh of Listowel was Dan Paddy Andy's physician and it was to him that Dan came when one of his eyes sustained an injury. After examining the eye and finding that Dan was in danger of losing the sight of it, Dr Johnny sent him to Tralee for a more detailed examination by the eye specialist Dr McNicholls. McNicholls succeeded in halting the decline in Dan's vision but only temporarily for, according to Dr Johnny, Dan later developed a cataract in the good eye and this, together with a deterioration in the bad eye, left him almost totally blind for several years before he died and ultimately contributed to a total loss of vision which greatly restricted his movements.

"The tragedy about his sight was that he didn't come to me in time," said Dr Johnny.

"When he first arrived in my surgery he studied my face for a long time before he spoke. 'You're Walsh the doctor,' he said, 'that's the son of Tom Walsh the draper.'

" 'That is correct,' I said.

" 'And,' said Dan, 'your grandfather was Seán Rua Walsh of Knockaclare and a Lyreacrompane man like myself, so there's no danger you'll be charging me as much as if I was a black stranger.' "

Dr Johnny also remembered "his beautiful mellow voice which reminded me of the actor and novelist Walter Macken. It was sonorous and deep and I confess to wasting more time on him than any other patient; and I ask you how could I ever charge him a fee when he spoke so charmingly of my forebears in Knockaclare. He did as much for my ego as ever I did for him."

Dan was in receipt of the blind pension for several years and there were some envious people in the locality who would from time to time write anonymous letters to the pensions' officer suggesting that Dan Paddy Andy wasn't in the least bit blind; that in fact he had superior sight when it suited him.

(It must be said here that Dan Paddy Andy feared nothing

on the face of the earth with the honourable exception of pensions' officers.)

"Why should he be getting two pensions, one blind and one old IRA" Dan's enemies would ask, "when he has the income from his farm, from his dancehall and from his matchmaking?" Actually Dan was entitled to two pensions. He had been an active member of the old IRA and there is plenty of medical evidence that his sight was seriously impaired.

Naturally these servants of the state would be obliged to investigate the complaints. The best way to describe Dan's sight at that particular time would be to say that it was mixed. In short there were times when he could see quite clearly and other times when he could not see at all. There is a popular story told about Dan concerning one of his encounters with a particular pensions' officer. One day he happened to be in a cinema in Tralee watching a matinee of *The Sign of the Cross* when the pensions' officer walked in and sat down beside him. Dan recognised him at once and as soon as the officer grew accustomed to the semi-darkness he had no difficulty in recognising Dan. Finally Dan spoke.

"Excuse me, sir," said he, "but is it any harm to ask will we be landing soon?"

"Landing where?" asked the pensions' officer irritably.

"Isn't this the bus for Castleisland?" Dan asked.

"It is, it is, and now will you shut up," said the pensions' officer who wanted to enjoy the film without further interruption.

Whatever about Dan's sight he was adept at answering questions posed by people he suspected of hidden hostility or ulterior motives. All his answers to queries from strangers were guarded.

"If there is one man that don't look like a pensions' officer," said Dan to his friend Dan Canty, "that man is a pensions' officer."

This may have been why Dan Paddy Andy over-reacted to any form of interrogation.

There was the time when two American priests came home on holiday to the nearby neighbourhood of Duagh. Both were monsignors but they discarded formal purple and black after a few days. Then one morning they decided to go fowling. They spent the first half of the day fruitlessly scouring the hills and boglands of the lower Stacks. After lunch they struck out for Lyreacrompane and for the abode of Dan Paddy Andy who was reputed to be a very knowledgeable man when it came to the locating of game.

"If there is a pheasant in the mountain," said a Duagh publican to the pair of clerics when they called for a snorter before lunch, "you may be sure that Dan Paddy Andy will put his paw down on him or if there is a grouse in the heather 'tis Dan will have his correct address; and as for hares," said he, "they does notify Dan when they moves from one form to another."

The two priests set out and in due course they arrived at Dan Paddy Andy's. Dan was sitting by the fire when they entered and although they were dressed in the apparel of fowlers he immediately knew who they were for it was common knowledge that they were in the neighbourhood. Dan was no great lover of the clergy. His name had been called from the pulpit too often.

"Could you tell us, like a good guy," said one of the clerics, "where we would find some game around here?"

"Game," said Dan and he pondered for a moment. "Game," he echoed before addressing himself fully to his visitors. "You will go back the way you came," said he, "and you will take the first turning to your right. Then you will take the next turn to the left until you come to a bridge with a hump on its back. After the bridge you will come to a cottage. There is a brace of widows fresh out of England in residence there and if 'tis game you're after you're at the right abode for by all accounts they're game to the tail."

While he always regretted his weak sight, Dan Paddy Andy was never a man to lament. He felt he was more than compensated in other ways.

"I can hear the grass growing," he used to say, "and there is no music like that. It is the first music that was ever heard and as for the feel of a thing if you was to bring me a horseshoe and hand it to me and say, 'Who made it?' I would know by the feel whether it was Coffey or Murphy or Dan Canty. Then if I heard talk a long ways off and if you was to ask me, 'Who is that coming the road down?' I'd put a name on whoever it was, no trouble at all, and I'd know the sound of one lorry from another or one car from another."

John Donnellan, chief engineer of the Board of Works, now retired, remembers Dan from the mid-Fifties when John was a young engineer based in Castleisland.

"He had extraordinary hearing," John Donnellan recalls. "He could distinguish the sound of my car engine from the many on the main street in Castleisland. I never refused him a lift. He was a great raconteur although I'm pretty sure he had given up matchmaking at that stage. His sight had almost failed him."

Dan Paddy Andy said, "That's what comes of not having to depend too much on the sight and 'twas a smart buck said when God closes one door he opens another."

Chapter 14

Dan was the first full-time matchmaker to emerge from the Stacks Mountains but he was by no means the first of his kind in rural Ireland. For generations before Dan's first successful match there had been a vital tradition of match-making in every part of the country and there were several published accounts of matchmaking procedures in rural Ireland long before Dan Paddy Andy O'Sullivan saw the light of day. As for instance there was Conrad Arensberg's "Country Marriage" in *The Irish Countryman*, a most perceptive piece well worth resurrecting. Arensberg writes: "Country marriage in Ireland follows an ancient and widespread pattern. It is called matchmaking and it is the sort of marriage of convenience involving parental negotiations and a dowry which is nearly universal in Europe. In Ireland its importance is such as to make it the crucial point of rural social organisation.

"To describe the match one has to sink one's teeth into the countryman's way of life. For the match is made up of many things. It unites transfer of economic control and advance to adult status. It is the only respectable method of marriage and the usual method of inheritance in the Irish countryside."

After the usual negotiations which involve a speaker or matchmaker, parents and friends, a meeting between the principals is arranged. Conrad Arensberg relates what he was told by a Clare farmer:

" 'If they suit one another, then they will appoint a day to come and see the land. If they don't no one will reflect on anybody but they will say he or she doesn't suit. They do not say plainly what is wrong. The day before the girl's people come to see the land, geese are killed, the house is whitewashed, whiskey and porter bought. The cows get a feed early so as to look good and maybe they get an extra cow in, if they want one. The next day comes the walking of the land. The young man stays outside in the street but he sends his best friend to show the girl's father around but sure the friend won't show him the bad points. If the girl's father likes the land he returns and there will be eating and drinking until the night comes on them. Then they go to an attorney next day and get the writings between the two parties and get the father of the boy to sign over the land.' "

Matchmaking procedures varied but slightly from place to place and from generation to generation. Here is how Dan Paddy Andy went about securing a wife for a farmer a few miles outside Castleisland. The time was 1940.

"I was scouring the country a long time for this buck. Age was the drawback. He said he was forty but he looked fifty. He had the grass of fourteen cows and there was a horse and pony. The land was dry and the cattle were in good condition. There was not much money there. 'Tisn't but he could not make out a wife himself locally but there was no fortune along of 'em and there was a sister in the house to be done for. She wanted £400 herself to marry into a place in Knocknagoshel.

"Around this time there was dribbles of news coming in to me about a farmer's daughter in Mountcoal between Listowel and Tralee. I told my man and informed him that all expenses from then on was to be borne by him and fair play he knocked a £5 note down on the table to be going on with. There was to be £1 a cow if there was a marriage followed by a blue back (£10 note) if there was a son out of the marriage and a fiver if there was a daughter. I went by horse and common cart to Mountcoal to see for myself and was well received. The next time I came I brought my man and he bought a bottle of whiskey in the Halfway Bar near Mountcoal. Again the time we had the bottle empty most of the bargaining was done. The girl got us the tay, sturdy but pleasant and mighty firm which is what they all want, man and boy. The next time I came I brought my man again and himself and the girl really took to one another and the £400 fortune was no obstacle.

"The following Sunday her father arrived along of his brother and an oul' warrior with a walking stick supposed to be a great judge of cattle. They walked the land. There wasn't a patch they didn't test and they looked over the cattle for hours but at the end of the day they announced that they were satisfied so we all went along to the Halfway

Bar owned by the Walsh's and we were as drunk as sticks. I didn't land home till cockcrow. I did well on that one. I was paid over my £14 on the spot and nine months to the day after the marriage didn't my buck raise a flag for all his years, a bull calf at that, so that was a tenner for Dan and didn't he register again a year after that, a dotey girl for me to get a £5 note into my hand."

Things weren't always so cut and dried and Dan had difficulties in other matches. The house might not be suitable. The location might be too lonely. There might be no young people in the district, no school and no church for miles, as we find in another part of Conrad Arensberg's thesis in *The Irish Countryman* during an interview with the same farmer from Inagh in the County Clare:

" 'The young lady's father asks the speaker what fortune do he want. He asks him the place of how many cows, sheep and horses is it? He asks what makings of a garden are in it; is there plenty of water or spring wells? Is it far in from the road or on it? What kind of a house is it, slate or thatch? Are the cabins good, are they slate or thatch? If it is too far in from the road he won't take it. Backward places don't grow big fortunes. And he asks, too, is it near a chapel and the school, or near town?' "

Dan Paddy Andy would be asked and expected to truthfully answer the same sort of questions.

"M'anam ón diabhal," said Dan, "if you held back you could land yourself in court for wilful deception. I fell across a fierce rogue myself an' I matchmaking for a decent girl from Cordal. I wasn't long on the road but I wasn't all that green either. Negotiations was well under way when I was consulted. If I was hired in time I may tell you 'twould have been stopped in time but better late than never as the man said. This girl was an only daughter with a fortune of £1,000 going with her and at the other side of the see-saw was this farmer from over near the county bounds, a mighty place by him by all accounts carrying twenty cows, two horses, à pony and a donkey, a fine house and outhouses, well located and wanting for nothing. We went along myself and the father of the girl and her brother. We walked the land and we examined the stock. No fault could we find and the man himself seemed to be alright except that he would look sideways if he was talking to you and on top o' that the hoor had a collar and tie and a tie pin and low shoes on a weekday, a bad omen, and hair oil running down the side of his face like 'twould be after raining on him. We got drunk in Scartaglin but not that drunk.

" 'Toughen a good while over this whatever else you do,' I advised the Cordal boys on the way home. 'This bird is fishier than my friend Jumpin' O'Hanlon and that's fishy enough for anything.'

"Ten days passed and who should I see in Castleisland and he enquiring after in-calf heifers but my buck from the county bounds and he dressed like an insurance inspector. Now, says I to myself, while the fox is on the prowl we'll have a look at his den. I was well armed this visit for hadn't I an ordnance map of the place in my pocket. I hired Sam Knight's hackney and away we went. I gave the best part of the morning walking the land and counting the stock. They were easy to count for all he had was eight miserable milch cows and a pony. The fine cows and horses we saw on our visit were the property of his brother-in-law, a low hoor like himself. The best of the farm he showed us wasn't his at all but belonged to an innocent neighbour who didn't know what was going on. We faced up to our man, myself and the Cordal girl's father and her brother and they had like to macerate him but for my coming between them. 'Twas the hair oil and the tie pin put me on to that buck in the first place.

"Many an innocent girl was done out of her rights by trickery. A lot of 'em, of course, thought themselves too smart and too grand to come to Dan. I was always able to stand over any commodity I put on the market, and so I should, for you can carry a soiled overcoat to the draper and demand a refund but who's going to give you a refund for a soiled wife? You can get a bigger size in a gansey if what the missus brought was too small or too loud but you'll have to wear a wife for life whether she suits or not.

"I'll tell you now I'd never blame a fellow for adding a neighbour's cow to his own to show a girl's father. So long as he didn't overdo it I'd make allowances. He might be after a bad winter or a thing and he might be in such a dreadful way for a woman that he'd stoop to anything and sure a good man would have no trouble making up the extra cow before he faced the altar. I knew men to walk ten or twelve miles of a night in order to steal a cow or two from a farmer that wouldn't starve for the loss of 'em. I would advise any man to let no one walk his land unless it was June or July when all land looks good and there's a shine on the worst of cattle."

Chapter 15

Word quickly spread that Dan Paddy Andy O'Sullivan had taken up the highly sensitive business of matchmaking. The expected few shook their heads as if to suggest that Dan would try anything to make money. The majority, however, were quick to agree that no man living in the Stacks Mountains was better qualified for the job.

Extraordinary knowledge was required if one were to be proficient at the business of matchmaking. What had happened in many instances up to this was that unscrupulous match-makers were determined, because of the substantial monetary recompense, to marry off couples at all costs, regardless of the compatability of the prospective bride and groom. This often resulted in disaster, and if the marriages were successful as often as not, it was not because of any special gifts the matchmakers possessed. A lot of heartbreak could be spared by not entrusting one's business to charlatans and pretenders. The margin for deceit could be totally eliminated if the matchmaker knew his business and was fully acquainted with the case histories of his clients.

Take the case of Dinny Doodawn which, of course, is not his real name at all.

Dinny was well into his forties before the way was clear for him to marry. He had a fine farm by local standards, a good house and money in the bank. The girl upon whom he cast a favouring eye was a fairly attractive damsel in her thirties who had been in Dan Paddy Andy's books for several years. Dan had repeatedly advised her against haste, assuring her that the right man would show up if she bided her time. It looked as if Dinny Doodawn would be that man.

Dan Paddy Andy, however, decided to do a spot of in-vestigating. Dinny Doodawn's neighbours told him nothing except what was favourable. This made Dan suspicious. He searched his memory and recalled vaguely that Dinny Doodawn was involved in some sort of household accident when he was a child. Apparently his mother was one morning boiling eggs for the breakfast while Dinny played near the doorway with a broken saucepan. When the eggs were boiled Dinny's mother threw the water out the door, but, alas, a spatter or two fell on Dinny's private part. No more was heard of the matter after some zinc ointment was applied.

Dan Paddy Andy decided to visit a man who worked in the Doodawn household at the time. The man was somewhat circumspect but Dan, nevertheless, deduced that all was not as it should be downstairs with Dinny Doodawn. He reported his findings to the girl who straightaway broke off negotiations. In despair Dinny Doodawn went to Dan Paddy Andy and begged him to find any woman at all to take the loneliness out of his life.

"You have money galore," Dan told him, "and my advice to you is to go to the best doctors who specialise in what ails you."

Dinny Doodawn took Dan Paddy Andy's advice. He wound up in London where a successful operation was performed. The result was that he returned home according to Dan "with a greatly improved undercarriage". He married the girl of his choice and they all lived happily ever after except Dan Paddy Andy who never received as much as a brown copper for the inestimable services he had rendered.

Dan was a much travelled man. He was also a known tracer who could pinpoint relationships, an essential accomplishment if he were to know the complete backgrounds of the men and women who would be facing for his abode in the years ahead.

From time to time Dr Johnny Walsh would send clients to Dan Paddy Andy.

"He didn't often succeed in arranging a marriage," said Dr Johnny, "but when he did the marriage was as successful as any. He was a mine of information as far as Lyreacrompane was concerned. He knew the medical history of every family. He could tell to the hour when they died and he knew how they died. He could trace relations to the third and fourth degree without a moment's hesitation. It was all part and parcel of his vocation, I know, but he was an extraordinary individual by any standard."

In his later years Dan Paddy Andy would hire Paddy Doran, a local farmer and taximan, to drive him around on the course of his duties. It was Paddy's great joy to listen to

Dan's recollections as he drove.

When Dan would dry up Paddy would get him going again by asking him about the people living in some particular house they passed. Paddy was amazed at Dan's knowledge. He could go back into the generations and give a complete picture of the family tree of every family in North Kerry and of many in Cork and Limerick as well. He knew the abodes and manner of living of every male and female who had left the household in question over a period of a hundred years. He knew the family characteristics, fads and political persuasions.

"If a lot of them knew," said Paddy, "what Dan knew about them, they'd hug the hearth and keep out of the lime-light."

Whenever Dan encountered communicative people from distant townlands and parishes he would pose question after question on the means, the health, the disposition, the wealth and mentality of every marriageable man and woman in the native place of the person being interrogated. Dan had no time for close-mouthed or secretive people and would even opt for the company of a babbling fool rather than be paired with an intelligent but inarticulate or taciturn individual. Intimate revelations about likely candidates for marriage were essential to Dan's enterprise.

One evening at the Cross of Renagown whilst a number of us were assisting him in the painting of the dancehall door Dan was approached by an elderly couple in a cob trap. It transpired that they were after information about a small farmer who had, some days before, proposed to their oldest daughter. Dan indicated that such information would not be forthcoming without a fee. Two single pound notes changed hands and Dan held forth.

"The man ye're enquiring about," said Dan, "has money in the bank to the tune of £300. He would be going on forty years of age and will be as bald as an apple again the time he's fifty for baldness runs in his breed. This daughter of yours will be in the family way in no time at all for all belongin' to him had the finest of population sticks."

"But," said the girl's mother, "rumour has it that he has a brother in the mental home and isn't there a fear that in the course of time he might go the same road himself?"

"No," said Dan. "There's no danger of that happening but you're right when you state that there is a brother 'behind' and although the man is wanting in wits there is no dúchas of that kind in the family for 'twas the big cattle fair in Glin of December the first that started his downfall. He was struck with a hames in the course of an argument and was rendered half-dead, poor fellow."

The elderly pair were well satisfied with themselves and allowed that the £2 was well spent.

When I myself was a gorsoon in the Stacks Dan Paddy Andy O'Sullivan was in his heyday and was besieged by bachelors and spinsters, not to mention widows and widowers, from one end of the day to the other. While outlining the assets of a client Dan might say "He have his own teeth" or "He's just after getting in his grinders" meaning that he had acquired new false teeth.

Astute and knowledgeable systematiser that he was, Dan Paddy Andy knew exactly how many teeth, parts of teeth and stumps of teeth occupied the mouths of his clients, as well as knowing the number of sets of false teeth, upper and lower. These were essential facts if the negotiations were to be successfully concluded. The absence of teeth or, worse still, black teeth, mitigated against the chances of middle-aged hopefuls.

Large gaps in the frontal array or that area of the teeth used for smiling were no asset either. Still if a man was otherwise presentable or was well-endowed with money and land the condition of his teeth was often overlooked. This could be dealt with after the knot was tied and he could be coaxed into going to the dentist in due course.

So the reader can now see that there was far more to the gentle art of matchmaking than the land and the stock it carried, more to it than the condition of the dwelling-house, the collocation of outhouses, dunghills, duck ponds and turf ricks. These were important and a dunghill too near a dwellinghouse could bring a premature end to otherwise successful negotiations. Dan stressed other important factors as well.

"As well as knowing the farm and the means of a man wanting to make the match, you'd have to know what kind of people he came from. Was there a history of sickness, was there mental disorders or bad blemishes? Was there a good life span and was there kind treatment of each other by the father and mother, and what way did the marriages of his sisters and brothers work out, that's if they married at all? Were they people that were given to tidiness and cleanliness or were they dirty and careless and maybe not even throw out the ashes?

"Then you'd have a lady wantin' to marry a townie and she not fit for a town. I knew this one that wanted me to make out a townie for her, any sort of a townie, because the poor cratur believed that townswomen did nothing but look out the window all day with the husband drawing tay and goodies to them. She thought this because she saw a fine lady looking out the window of a house in the Square in Listowel one evening after the races when there was fierce crowds about. Of course, if the oinseach was to go to Listowel the day after the races she wouldn't find many looking out their windows, but that's what she thought and it couldn't be knocked out of her head. A fair share of ladies wanted to marry townies because they found the back of beyond too lonesome, forgetting a town could be just as lonesome and more lonesome I'll engage you.

"Before I would consent to sanction a match, any kind of a match now, I would want to know the partners like the back of my hand. Of course, the chances would be that I would know them and theirs anyway, but if a client came from far away I'd often find myself in a quandary and I might ask for references from a priest or a schoolmaster. 'Tisn't but this could catch you out too, for what is to stop one trickster from writing out a reference for another trickster. No, you'd want a spy in the camp and you'd nearly want to go to the place yourself and enquire around nice and cute, for if they knew what you were up to there is no way you'd get a straight answer.

"You'd feel your way around, ask here and there at fairs and the like. Oh you'd put together their alphabet alright if you weren't in too much of a hurry. That's another thing now I'd be wary of — when they'd be in too much of a hurry. Hurry botches every job and 'tis no different in my trade. I do always be suspicious of anyone in a hurry and I may tell you I'd be just as suspicious of a body that would delay too much.

"A great thing when a client came from foreign parts was to make out a Civic Guard from the area. That time no sane Guard would refuse porter and for a few pints you'd be well filled-in about a body's character. Of course, with certain people you'd never know anything for there was nothing to be known. You'd hear nothing good or nothing bad, and if you want my opinion about them sort of people, I would say go around 'em like you'd go around a boghole. If they're that close they're best avoided. I wouldn't hold it against a man if he spent a tamall in jail. There's many a man wrongfully jailed and there's many outside that should be inside and I could give you a list of their names longer than any litany. Anyway devil the much harm does a while inside do and there's many a man all the better for it. You'll never find the real villains inside of a jail.

"Another thing that happens after one lady marries into a place a good ways from her own home is she would be followed in time by a younger sister or a niece. When a woman is lucky in a place one of her own is sure to follow in the hopes that they'll be lucky too; and having an aunt or a sister is a good start, for they'll have company if they get lonely, although it's my experience that a marriage fares better when the pair has no recourse to relations and has to sort things out for themselves. Women especially, if they know there's a refuge contagious, will always be running there instead of making up in the natural way after a quarrel. The natural way is the only way in the long run. Any couple that has spent a lifetime together will tell you that.

"I'll tell you another thing too for no charge and this is it. Better for a man fall in line with a woman than be expecting her to fall in line with him. 'Tis a deal easier for a man to skip into step. You won't drill a woman for long so better keep the step with her. Give her the handling of the money as well and you'll never want, no matter how hard the times."

Chapter 16

The one man who was closer to Dan Paddy Andy than any other was Dan Canty, the blacksmith who plied his ancient trade at his forge in Carrigcannon near the Four Elms pub where mine host is Jimmy Roche and whose illustrious and poetry-loving father, the late Al Roche, was mine host before him. After the war tractors began to appear more and more in the Stacks so that Dan Canty's smithy was out of commission more often than not.

"I decided to do a bit of hackney work to supplement my earnings," said Dan, "so I bought a second-hand Prefect from Guard Dwyer of Moyvane. It had a historical registration, *IN 1014*, which was the year Brian Boru beat the Danes at the battle of Clontarf if we can believe what we're told. I got it for £100. I suppose it would be £3,000 or £4,000 today. I got decent luck money too from Dwyer.

"I got along well with Dan most of the time and I drove him everywhere for several years until he sacked me one evening. 'Twas well coming to me for, God knows, he gave me warnings galore. The trouble with me was that I couldn't help laughing out loud whenever I would listen to Dan describing the qualities of a client. There would be Dan and he dead serious, talking for all he was worth and putting the best face he could on his side of things. Then he'd say something that I thought to be funny and I'd burst out laughing. There was no way I could be stopped. The more I laughed the blacker would get Dan's face.

" 'Quit out of here, you danged fool,' Dan would shout but I'd only laugh all the more. 'Quit, you hoor, or I'll lay a boot on you,' Dan would shout, but I couldn't be stopped. 'Canty,' said Dan to me and we driving home one evening through Tooreenmore between Headley's Bridge and Castleisland, 'I'll have to dispense with your services. You're going around now for years with your mouth open and you laughing like an ape, you danged amadán. Don't you know matchmaking is a serious business and that my job is hard enough without you making it any harder.'

"That was the last time I drove Dan but we were always close friends and I continued to play the accordeon whenever I was invited to the Renagown hall. To tell the truth I was the wrong kind of assistant for a matchmaker."

According to Dan Canty, matchmaking was Dan Paddy Andy's first love. It was often a highly complicated business as shall be seen from the following incident described by Dan Canty.

The nearer the client to Dan Paddy Andy's Renagown home, the less willing was he to lend his professional services. Faraway clients were easier to handle and no reduction in fees was expected as would be the case with a near neighbour. However, Dan was never a man to turn his back on a neighbour's plight and when he was approached by a farmer who lived less than a mile and a half away he responded like the true Christian that he was.

Dan Canty was hired to transport the principals. His hire would be paid in advance by the farmer as would any and all expenses such as drink and food together with Dan's fee, which was a little less than usual because of his friendship with the farmer in question.

On such occasions Dan Canty would be expected to shave and wear his best clothes although he would not be asked to play any part in the proceedings.

"I could be judged by the way you look," Dan Paddy Andy told him, "so spruce up like a good man and put some sort of a flower in your lapel don't the neighbours think 'tis in mourning we are."

The least happy-looking member of the expedition was the farmer, but this could be because he was footing the bill with no assurance of a successful conclusion from his investment.

The farmer had two sons in their late twenties, both of whom were anxious to get married. To the older son would go the farm but he had no hope of bringing in a woman until the second son departed. The second son had no fortune, not a brown shilling to call his own, so that his chances of marrying into a farm were slender, to say the least.

In addition, the father had a brother in the house, a dour oul' fellow in his fifties who had a fortune of £400, not a bad handful in those impecunious days.

Dan Paddy Andy was consulted and it transpired that he

knew a woman in the Limerick direction, Abbeyfeale to be exact, who might marry the uncle. She was well on in the years or, as Dan might say, "She was greying." She was an only daughter, however, and was possessed of a fine farm.

The party set out for West Limerick in Dan Canty's Ford Prefect after first mass of a Sunday morning in the fall of the year. They arrived at their destination in the mid-afternoon. The party consisted of Dan, the penniless second son and the uncle with the £400.

"Don't you come in," said Dan to the second son, "but let you take up your position by yon window and don't move from that spot."

The second son did as he was bade and sat himself on a low wall which fronted the house.

In the house Dan and the uncle were well received. The bottle was produced and after a while the elderly parents of the spinster announced that they were pleased with the uncle. The money was right as well, so all seemed fair set for a wedding.

The kettle which had been put down at the commencement of the negotiations proceeded to sing merrily and soon the table presented an array of choice edibles.

"Why don't the boy outside come in?" the spinster asked after she had taken careful stock of him through the kitchen window.

"Shy," Dan Paddy Andy answered.

"Would he not come in for a mouthful of tay?" asked the mother.

"The only way," said Dan, "that he'll take tay is to carry tay out to him."

"Then tay shall be carried out," said the man of the house. All duly sat at the table, saving the spinster who put together a trayful of edibles for the boy without. Out with her then and, like the kindly fellow he was, the boy expressed his gratitude and spoke as follows:

"Sit up here," said he, "'till we pass the time of day."

"I will a dale," said she, "and my future husband waiting inside for me."

Nevertheless, she stood for a while as they made ordinary observations about the weather, the crops and the price of milk. Their talk ranged further to the general condition of the country and the world at large until there was no more to be said unless it was to be something of a personal nature. Forestalling such a possibility, the spinster gathered herself and went indoors, where she sat with her visitors and family until the meal was consumed.

"Well now," said Dan Paddy Andy as he looked happily into a glass of whiskey which had been thrust into his hand, "it has been a good day's work without doubt and I'll propose a toast to that."

All lifted their glasses and swallowed.

"And yourself, Missie," Dan put the question to the spinster, "I take it that you're happy and content with yourself in the heel of this happy evening?"

The spinster seemed reluctant to answer. A knowing smile spread across Dan's face.

"Speak now," said he, "or forever hold your peace."

Still the spinster remained silent but her face was serious as though she were resolving some very serious matter in her mind.

"A dumb priest never got a parish," Dan suggested, hoping that she might say her say. Finally Dan grew tired of this shilly-shallying and he addressed her bluntly.

"Are you or are you not content with your choice?" he demanded. Dan rose from his seat and began to button his coat. He stood in the centre of the kitchen awaiting an answer.

"No," said the spinster after a while, "I am not content."

A cry of despair rose from the uncle whilst the parents exchanged baleful glances. Were they to be straddled with this wilful daughter for the remainder of their days? Would the cry of a child never gladden their hearts or the hand of a child hold theirs in walks through the land.

It was a lonesome prospect.

"And pray," said Dan, "what do you find wrong with this man alongside me?"

"There's nothing at all wrong with him," said the spinster, "except that I'd rather the boy outside on the wall."

This astonishing statement was greeted with shocked silence. If the truth were told, of course, Dan Paddy Andy was not shocked at all. Was it not he who had instructed the young man to park himself in the most favourable

74

position outside the window, a position where he would be seen by the spinster.

"He hasn't a halfpenny to his name," the uncle put in suddenly.

"True," said Dan.

"'Tis him I want," said the spinster.

"Go in the Room," Dan told her, "and come down when you're called; and you," he turned to the uncle, "go in the haggard till you hear a holler."

When Dan found he had the kitchen to himself he addressed the parents.

"Money he might not have," Dan said, "but there is no scarcity of strength or youth which is more than his uncle has. You may be sure that there will be children laughing and crying in a short time if this young man is to take up residence here."

The parents considered what Dan said and, after a while, they nodded their heads in agreement.

On the way home in the trap, that night, the uncle started to cnawvshawl.

"Houl', you hoor," said Dan, "there's a woman as has been watching your nephew this while will be rightly annoyed now that he's promised. She's young and tender and, if 'twas for nothing else, she'd marry you for spite."

In this manner, Dan Paddy Andy killed two birds with one stone and made himself a double day's hire in the process.

Chapter 17

Dan Paddy Andy, as readers will have deduced by now, was a man with a comprehensive sense of humour. This was a very necessary adjunct to his mental and physical surival in those grim years during and following the Economic War.

When, in 1932, Eamon de Valera became Taoiseach of the Free State whose foundation he had always opposed with consistent bitterness, his first major act was to declare economic war upon Britain.

Many Irish farmers still owed huge sums to the British government in return for loans made in order to purchase their own lands from the former Ascendancy classes. De Valera contended that no further payments should be made on the grounds that the lands in question had been stolen from the Irish people in the first place.

British retaliation was swift and severe. Heavy tariffs were placed on all Irish goods entering the country and, of course, the Irish government did the same to English imports.

The real victim of the Economic War, which was to last for several years, was the Irish farmer who had geared himself towards the production of beef for export to Britain.

Mercifully there was a solution in 1938 when Chamberlain announced that he was willing to accept £10,000,000 in cash from the Free State government in settlement of outstanding land-purchase loans. Part of the deal was that all British naval personnel would be removed from the three remaining British bases in Ireland. The Economic War was a major blunder, but it can be argued that de Valera more than made up for the mistake by keeping the Free State out of World War II.

Dan Paddy Andy O'Sullivan idolised Eamon de Valera and would even have been prepared to take up arms in defence of the Economic War policy. There is no doubt but that de Valera ran Ireland single-handed from 1932 to 1948 and in the process earned extraordinary devotion and loyalty from his many followers.

The year that followed the ending of the Economic War

was a grim one for Europe and the real beginning of a dour six year struggle for European supremacy. It was in the spring of this year that Dan Paddy Andy decided to hold his first supper dance.

Prior to this momentous occasion there had been a falling-off in attendance in the Renagown hall due to a rumour which circulated freely throughout the Stacks Mountains at the time. Dan Paddy Andy was said to be in the Pope's black books and was due to be excommunicated or visited by some other form of canonical punishment at any time. Dan always maintained that the rumour was started by a rival impresario but he could never prove this.

In addition to the rumour there were too many counter attractions in the district and new cinemas were appearing in increasing numbers in the surrounding towns. There were also numerous crossroads and platform dances although these were destined to vanish from the scene after the war. Then there were the other local dancehalls as, for instance, the famous Dan Connie's Loft in the nearby village of Knocknagoshel. There was a new and extremely popular hall in Mountcollins and another very popular hall at Kilconlea outside Abbeyfeale while every contiguous town had at least two major dancehalls and often more. Competition then was tough and new measures were desperately required if the Renagown hall was to survive. The continuing attacks from the clergy were no help either.

Up to this time, Dan had tried everything from singing competitions to walzing competitions and when these began to pall he was obliged to rack his brains for alternative attractions.

"The only sort of a dance I never had," said Dan to his neighbour Joe Sheehy, "was a fancy dress dance."

"Why not?" Joe Sheehy asked.

"Because," said Dan, "I would always like to be know who would be coming into my hall and this part of the world as you know has its own fair share of blackguards. Bad as my sight is and dark as the night might be I would always be able to make these fellows out and show them the road. If I was to hold a fancy dress dance how would I know them behind the disguises? M'anam ón diabhal, they'd wreck myself and wreck the hall."

Dan had a long list of known blackguards who were banned from Renagown. A ban would be of little use unless it was enforceable. Dan had no trouble enforcing his. Snowstorms were his biggest dread. There was no townland within a radius of five miles that didn't boast its own blackguard. Consequently when there was heavy snow there was no way of travelling afar and they were left with no other choice but the out of bounds Renagown hall. Since admittance was out of the question they had nothing better to do but bombard the dancehall with showers of snowballs. Many of these contained stones, bolts, washers and nails. Dan was left with no option but to call off the dance.

Because of the space limitations of the Renagown hall Dan could only afford a prize of £1 for the winners of the competitions with 5s. for the runners up whereas in Listowel, Castleisland and Abbeyfeale there were silver cups and cash prizes of £10, £5 and £3 for first, second and third.

Neither could Dan afford any of the more popular bands such as Darky Devine or the Kingdom Showband or Locke, Herrity and Hayes or the Devon Dance Band or Arthuro's Band from Listowel or Bunny Dalton's popular combination from the same town. All Dan could afford was one accordeon player and this was nearly always Tom Doran or Dan Canty although sometimes Ebbie Somers of Carrigcannon played at Renagown as did Dan Brosnan of Dromadamore.

"There was no stage in the Renagown hall," Tom Doran recalls, "but if there was a big crowd Dan would put me on a chair in the right hand corner and nail a deal board from wall to wall so that I was cut off from the dancers."

The four mentioned were all accomplished musicians but they never earned more than 5s. for any night's work. A half-crown was the going rate until 1938.

"Five shillings was a lot before the war," Tom Doran explained. "Woodbines were 2d. for a packet of five. You'd get a fine bottle of superfine brilliantine or any other kind of hair oil for 2d. Players or Gold Flake or Afton were 6d. for a packet of ten. You'd buy a bun bigger than your first for a penny and you'd get as much gallon sweets for a halfpenny as would keep you sucking all day."

"You could get rotten drunk on 5s.," Dan Canty recalls, "or you could go to McCarthy's restaurant in Castleisland

and get four of the finest dinners you ever ate for 5s., plenty fresh meat, vegetables, floury spuds with a cup of tea and a bun after. Cripes, man, I knew fellas that got married for 5s."

The idea for the supper dance came to Dan while he was seated by the fire one night reading the *Irish Press*, aided by powerful spectacles. Dan never bought the *Irish Press* except when he went to town. It often took him the best part of a week to get through it. The *Irish Press* was his paper and to no other publication, *The Kerryman* apart, would he subscribe or believe in until the day he died.

His politics were Fianna Fáil. In fact he once ran unsuccessfully for the Kerry County Council on the Fianna Fáil ticket. The isolation of his Renagown headquarters militated against any possible chance of his winning. There was also an established Council member in the area. Dan's entry into the political arena was also frowned upon by many of Fianna Fáil's leading lights in the constituency. He was, in short, beaten before he began. His friends insisted that his heart wasn't in it and having let his name go forward he immediately regretted it.

While perusing the pages of his favourite paper on the night in question Dan was engrossed by an account of a supper dance which had been held in Mallow on the previous Saturday night. This was the Duhallow Hunt Ball. Slowly the idea dawned upon him that this might be the solution to his problems, a ball of his own with supper thrown in. Since there was no hunt in the Stacks Mountains he could not very well call it a hunt ball so he decided upon the Renagown and Lyreacrompane Annual Dinner Dance. Dancing nine to three. Midnight supper.

Straightaway he set to work. He had bills printed by Cuthbertson of Listowel. He engaged Tom Doran and told him to be prepared for an all-night session. The normal admission fee would have to be raised for the occasion, so Dan decided that instead of the usual 3d. an admission price of 10d. should be charged.

"You'll never get 10d. out of 'em," Tom Doran cautioned.

"If the 10d.'s are there," said Dan, "we'll get them and if they're not there we can't get them."

Supper was to consist of white bread and jam and tea

seved in pannies. White bread was, of course, another name for bakers' bread which at the time was a luxury in country places. In those days every country house had its half sack of flour in the corner or in the bin and the daily bread was, therefore, always home-made.

The jam was simply known as red jam, which, in reality, was either strawberry, raspberry, plum or mixed fruit. The name given to marmalade in those uncomplicated times was white jam and to blackcurrant, black jam. The jam used by Dan Paddy Andy on the night of the big supper dance was of the mixed fruit variety. It was cheapest and it spread easily. It came in a large tin bucket from Castleisland. The bread also came from Castleisland. This consisted of several batches of loaves known as tiles. They came in a tea-chest. There were twelve tiles and a crusted end tile to each batch.

Luckily for Dan the night was fine. It was the beginning of September. A week earlier the Second World War had officially begun after Britain and France had declared war on Germany. As soon as darkness fell Dan took up his position at the door of the dancehall and waited hopefully for whatever business might be forthcoming.

The stars danced in the sky the moment light took its leave and promptly on the stroke of nine the band arrived. The band had a few drinks taken for the purpose of steadying its nerves. Tom Doran recalls that he made the sign of the cross on his forehead as he entered the hall. If the dance was a flop it would be a financial disaster for Dan Paddy Andy.

Immediately, as if this were the cue for which everybody had been waiting, boys and girls began to appear from the shadows under the thorn trees and whins which flanked the four roads composing the cross. A number of older couples who hadn't attended a dance for years would show up later on.

The girls went in first, handing their money to Dan as they passed him by. Each coin was carefully checked before admission was granted. The method was simple. Dan would bite every piece with his powerful teeth and if it passed this test he would then weigh it carefully in his left hand before sampling its flavour by the simple process of sucking it. As soon as the girls had entered, the band got things off to a lively start with "Let him go, let him tarry". No one took the floor, of course, for the first dance but when Tom struck the first chords of "Loch Lomond", the girls partnered each other and were content to while away the time in this fashion until the boys arrived on the scene and asked the damsels of their choice on to the floor.

As always the boys were reluctant to enter. They would stand huddled in small groups around the entrance waiting for one of the more daring bucks to make the first move. Dan would make his famous announcement at this stage.

"Plenty cotton inside lads. Come on in now."

There would be a sheepish reaction at first accompanied by shuffling and leering. They would push and shove each other forward until exhorted once more by Dan.

"Come on in boys. Plenty cotton here." Dan extended his hands in welcome and one by one the young men entered. Later the older people came, married couples and the more advanced bachelors and spinsters. With the married couples came young boys and girls not yet in their teens. Everybody danced. There was no age limit. At midnight the hall was packed to capacity.

From time to time, at Dan's request, a batch of people would leave for a while to make way for another batch who might have been waiting outside. It was a happy time, but most important of all, man, woman and child were involved. The occasion embraced the whole community and this was a social outlet for which rural Ireland sorely pined in the pre-war period.

While Dan had been looking to the door others of mischievous intent had eaten half the bucket of jam which Dan had in a cupboard at the rear of the hall. The blackguards replaced what they had eaten with wet turf mould and smoothed the surface carefully after they had given the mould and jam a thorough mixing. In the poor light of the hall's only paraffin lamp no one would notice the difference, or so they hoped.

Eventually suppertime came. A few local women, some of them relations of my own, had boiled a large skilletful of water so that tea was ready in no time at all. There were several sittings. The sliced bread was smeared with jam and handed out all round. Tea was served in tin pannies and the colouring came from an enamel bucket which stood nearby.

In jig time jaws were working overtime and bit by bit the full tea-chest of bread was seen to disappear.

In the end everybody had enough and there was no complaint, not a\single one. Not a crumb of the bread was left, nor was there as much jam as would colour the back of a threepenny piece. The blackguards who had done the mixing waited for the fireworks and were seen to be hugging themselves in joyous anticipation of things to come. As the night wore on, however, nothing happened. The time came for the last dance and those who couldn't dance inside the hall danced outside under a full moon and a sky full of glinting stars. There wasn't a puff of wind and the air was as crisp and as clear and as rare as the finest champagne. The heavens themselves were mute in tribute to this delightful occasion. Romance blossomed among the young folk and old fancies stirred themselves anew in the breasts of those who should never have allowed such fancies to hibernate.

It was a great time for young and old, a great time for the countryside and for the rustic way of life. It was a time for pride in what people could make of themselves if only they would remember that life can be great as often as one wishes to make it great but also that it can only be great while it is possessed of dignity. The Renagown supper dance would be followed by many others from time to time but none had the airy innocent quality of that first rapturous night when cheek to cheek dancing bloomed again and when Tom Doran played as he never played before in his life. The stars paled in the frosty heavens before the dancing ended and when Tom Doran stood on his chair to play the National Anthem everybody sang the words and everybody held hands in peace and friendship.

That memorable night also showed that the people of Ireland were hardier then than they are now. After the consumption of several pounds of turf mould there was not a single case of sickness reported the following day or any day thereafter. If it happened now they would probably all be hospitalised with food poisoning.

Unquestionably this was one of Dan Paddy Andy's finest hours and it showed as if it ever needed showing that the Stacks Mountains and more particularly the country of Renagown would have been a far less colourful place if he had never seen the light of day. When Dan was complimented on his initiative the following day all he said was, "Anything is better than going up in the Room and hanging your head."

Chapter 18

"We had tay and thing in the Room." This derogatory catchcry was popular with conveniently shortsighted townies freshly returned from visits to their country cousins. What made it all the more derogatory was that these self same townies were only a bare step removed from being country-folk themselves.

The Room is now almost a thing of the past in country places although in the older farmhouses it is still something of a shrine. It was, in Dan Paddy Andy's negotiations, an inherent part of the bargaining procedure. The question would always be asked sooner or later. "Have they a Room?" If the answer was in the affirmative it was a decided asset. If not it frequently put paid to an aspirant's chances there and then.

It was possibly the major status symbol in rural Ireland next to having a priest in the family. There was a time when it was looked upon as the inner sanctum of the rustic household, the venerable repository of all that was ancient and respectable. It was the treasure house for those relics of oul' decency which successive wives had managed to hoard over the years. The odd thing was that it was never used by members of the house themselves. It was reserved for visiting Yanks, clerics and other dignataries and as Dan Paddy Andy was once paradoxically heard to say, "A house without a Room is no house."

It was specially reserved for station breakfasts and for the hearing of confessions prior to the station mass which was generally held in the kitchen. The priest would sit with his elbows resting upon the mahogany table, his head averted, whilst the humble penitents approached, one by one, to be shrived of their transgressions.

After mass and communion the visiting priest would sit at the head of the creaking mahogany table on a plush-covered chair. Around him would sit the parish clerk and the head of the house, together with the more substantial farmers and tradesmen of the townland.

They sat erect and uncomfortable, completely out of place. Women never sat at the station table. Their place was to serve and this they were honoured and delighted to do. Satined and cottoned and scrubbed as clean as whistles they came from and went to the Room with choice edibles and steaming teapots of freshly made tea.

The parish clerk acted as a buffer between the priest and his parishioners. The conversation was nearly always stunted except when Dan Paddy Andy was present. Priest or no priest, Dan always spoke his mind. When the priest departed, the Room was immediately vacated and the men removed themselves to more natural surroundings such as the farthest corner of the kitchen from the hearth or the vicinity of the front door whether inside or out. Here they would quickly reassume their rightful rôles as ordinary countryfolk, light their pipes and swallow the stout or whiskey without which the station breakfast would not be complete. Several years might well pass before the Room would be called into use again.

In the home where I was reared and countrified in the Stacks there was such a Room but neither myself nor any other of the younger members of the household were allowed within striking distance of it. Nearly all worthwhile Rooms had a large mahogany table in the centre, several plush-covered chairs, a sideboard covered with American marriage photographs and ancient coloured glass vases, often cracked. The table was covered with a plush cloth, usually dark green or wine red in colour. Sometimes there would be must and dust and damp all over the place. Over the fire on the mantel was the inevitable pair of plaster chows and on the wall above the mantel was an enlarged photograph of the father and mother of the present incumbent. Real stuffed shirts they seemed, the woman in her black satin brooched blouse and himself with a stiff collar, a waxed moustache and the hair on his head plastered to his poll with the most consistent of pomades. A starched white collar bit deeply into his neck and over his heart he held a topper or bowler provided specially for the occasion by the photographer.

There was no semblance of a smile on the face of either. Rather did they look reproachfully down on those who dared to breach the holy of holies which was the Room.

She was seated on a plush-covered chair with her hands neatly folded on her lap whilst he stood ramrod-like behind with a bearing that conveyed all the majesty of a highly respected local squire instead of the shy, unlettered, small farmer that he really was.

In the drawers of the sideboard would be old letters from America, neatly bundled, station tablecloths, other linens and candlesticks together with cruets and all the paraphernalia which contributed to the laying out and waking of the dead. There were mortuary cards and moth-balls and broken briar pipes as well as pocket watches whose movement had expired under the ministrations, some-times surprisingly successful, of calloused agricultural hands.

In glaring contrast behind the closed doors of the side-board would be a mighty earthenware chamber pot with some form of sylvan scene enriching its outer body and the most ornate of handles extending from its bulging side. It might never have been used although it might have been pressed into service when the Yanks were home on holiday or when visiting females such as nuns and even doughtier matriarchs were caught short.

Next to the chamber pot in order of importance would be the china half-set which dominated the antique glass case, which also contained a variety of dishes, casseroles and drinking glasses, all called into use at the station breakfast or recurring wakes and otherwise preserved for the nurse and doctor when those worthies called to assist new arrivals into the world and to usher elderly occupants out.

Near us in Renagown at the time lived a boy who once confessed that he had never seen the inside of their Room. It was always kept locked by his mother probably because hidden in a jug or vase or cup there was the rates money or a blueback or two reserved for special occasions like Listowel Races or the Pattern of Knocknagoshel on 15 August.

When Dan Paddy Andy entered such a room he made a thorough inventory of its contents. To do this properly he would, because of his failing sight, take Tom Doran or some other observant acolyte along with him.

Dan once invited me to accompany himself and Tom Doran when he called to a farmhouse about three miles from Renagown Cross. He had successfully matched the daughter of the house and it was time for the collection of his fee. When we entered the house, despite Dan's protests we were shown at once to the Room and invited to take seats.

Dan's protests, by the way, were only token. He wished to give the impression that he wasn't worthy of such an honour. Like Caesar he was a plain, blunt man the same as themselves. There was the usual mahogany table in the centre of the Room and I was amazed to see displayed on its centre an outsize earthenware chamber pot filled with paper flowers made by passing tinker women. In those times tinker folk rarely resorted to begging. The men were nearly all competent tinsmiths, makers of tin pannies ideal for children or for the bog. In addition they made gallons and saucepans to measure whilst the females contributed to the family upkeep by creating beautiful paper flowers. As soon as we were seated Dan rubbed his hands along the plush of his chair before rising to feel his way around. The owners of the house would have been preparing tea or stronger drinks in the kitchen. Tom and myself directed Dan from one object to another until he was familiar with the Room's contents.

"There's money here, Tomáisín," Dan addressed himself to Tom Doran after he resumed his seat.

"How can you say that, Dan" Tom prompted, "and you as blind as a bat?"

"I smell it," Dan replied. He proved to be right for after a while we were presented with glasses of whiskey for Dan and Tom Doran and wine for myself. Dan set an outrageous figure on his services pointing out that there had been several others interested in his client but that he had fought tooth and nail for the daughter of the house. Haggling followed but in the end Dan came away with ten pounds more than he had anticipated. He left the house with three bluebacks in his pocket and a triumphant smile on his face.

"Show me the Room," he said to Tom Doran, "and I'll tell you their value."

We see, therefore, that the Room was an important aspect of country life. It was also a hallowed area for contemplation or for those who were obliged, because of shyness or simple backwardness or some deep, secret hurt, to seek refuge from time to time there. We see what Dan was driving at when he said at the conclusion of the supper dance:

"Anything is better than going up in the Room."

Chapter 19

The trickiest, toughest and most unlikely match ever made by Dan Paddy Andy O'Sullivan was completed in the fall of the year of 1943, a black time in Europe but a good enough time in Ireland where money was scarce but where the vast majority had enough to eat.

Churchill and Roosevelt met Chiang Kai-Shek in Cairo and Stalin in Teheran. In Renagown, Dan Paddy Andy met a widow who was to test his capacity for matchmaking to the utmost. Dan was well established as a matchmaker at this stage of his career and had over a hundred marriages notched up on a stout cudgel which he kept near the fireplace in case burglars or others of mischievous intent might invade his home during the night.

Dan was sitting by the fire late one night reading the *Irish Press* when there was a gentle but unexpected knock at the door. Dan opened it and there entered a woman he had never seen before. He bade her sit by the fire where he took stock of her. She had a fortyish look about her. She was small and prim. She was also reasonably attractive. Kate O'Brien, Dan never called his wife anything else, set about wetting a mouthful of tea. When this was swallowed the woman related her tale. She had put more than seven miles behind her that night on a rickety bicycle. Several years before she had lost her husband. He went down under pneumonia. Tragedy struck a second time when she lost her only daughter, a little girl of five, to the plague of diphtheria which mercilessly swept the countryside in the awful spring of 1937. In Kerry alone there were nearly a hundred deaths at the hands of this grim reaper.

Dan sympathised with the woman and congratulated her on bearing up so well. She thanked him and explained that she would like to get married again to a man who was fond of the road, who wouldn't be mooning around her all the time. Dan thought this strange but she told him she did not wish to grow too fond of a man a second time. She did not want her heart broken again.

"What you ask," Dan told her, "is almost impossible. I take it you're at a crabbed age yourself and on this account will be wanting a chap of the same years or thereabouts. At this age a man is sure to have his wild oats sown and won't be too anxious for the road. The hearth would be more in his line and that is as it should be."

Before she left, however, she managed to wring a promise out of him that he would find the kind of man she wanted.

"Well," said Dan, "if he's in this side of the world I'll find him, and if he's not, that will be the end of it."

Months passed and the woman called again. She had a tidy little house and a modest farm. She wasn't short of money but she was growing anxious. The winter had arrived and it was colder than usual.

Dan racked his brains in desperation. It was the most unusual pucker with which he had ever been confronted.

"I see light," he informed the woman. "I declare to God but I see light."

She smiled. It was the first time she indulged in one.

"Would you marry a travelling man?" Dan asked.

"Is it a tinker you mean?" she asked.

"If you like," said Dan, "that's what I mean. Take him or leave him but there's no other will suit your case. There is one of the Black Carty's," Dan went on, "who lost his woman four years ago. He's a fine cut of a man and about your own age which I would say is closer to forty than thirty."

The woman was agreeable but Dan was not to contact Carty till the January horse fair in Listowel. The match was made after the couple were introduced to each other. Carty spent the winter and the first half of spring with his new woman, but the minute the buds started to show themselves on the thorn bushes he took to the road and hide nor light of him wasn't seen till the wild geese started to wing their way south with the coming of winter. The marriage, such as it was, worked well. When Carty was out he was out but, fair dues to him, when he was home he stayed at home. The only time he stirred from her side during his home periods was to the occasional horse fair in Tralee, Castleisland or Listowel. He would return from these expeditions full of fight and porter but, experienced woman that she was, she took him nice and handy and there was never any trouble.

Time passed and she bore him a son, a laughing, black-haired, daft-eyed bundle of mischief, the dead stamp of the father. To balance the scales she bore him a daughter the following year. The daughter took after herself. In the late spring and through the full length of the summer and autumn she missed Carty but as time went by she took him as she found him. Then the poor fellow got a cramp in his stomach after the horse fair of Cahirmee. It was the prelude to a monstrous coronary which felled him forever less than a week later. She missed him for a while but because she hadn't had him by her side all the time she didn't miss him that much. The children grew up hale and hearty and were as well-behaved as children could be.

Again Dan Paddy Andy had struck a blow against loneliness and proved that he was equal to any problem regardless of how difficult that problem might be.

Chapter 20

Dan Paddy Andy had another case which he considered one of his most difficult assignments. This was to find a woman for the grandson of an old friend of his grandfather's from the Cork side. The man in question was of a most poisonous disposition. He was desired in no company and his chief pastime was talking to himself. This might not have been too bad if the talk was of a pleasant nature. It was anything but because the unfortunate man was always giving out about one thing or another. If the day was fine it was too hot and if the price of cattle was good he would speak of a time when it was not good. For years the poor fellow had tried to find a wife and in the end according to Dan, "He had come to such a pass that he'd marry a tailor's dummy in order to have someone to be looking at."

In despair his neighbours came to Dan Paddy Andy. They came in a hackney car, four respectable farmers, and they landed outside Dan's door just as he was returning from last mass in Castleisland. They introduced themselves and acquainted Dan with their problem.

"Face around, now let ye," said Dan, "and turn the bonnet of yeer vehicle in the direction of Castleisland. This could turn out to be a thirsty job and we'd want to be where there's medicine for dry throats."

The Corkmen got the message and in no time at all they were on their way to the headquarters of the Moonlighters, which was the name Dan Paddy Andy used when referring to the town in question. As bona fide travellers they had no difficulty in finding a public house to accommodate them and in no time at all they were seated in front of a blazing fire drinking hot whiskeys while Dan listened to the full circumstances surrounding the case. He allowed all four and the hackney driver to have their spake and during all that time not as much as a single word was heard from the attentive Dan Paddy Andy. He was a faithful subscriber to the views of Polonius, "Give every man thine ear but few thy tongue."

Finally, when several whiskies had been consumed and all the talk exhausted, Dan gave a short resumé of the combined reveiations which had been disclosed to him.

"We have before us," said Dan, "a man given to bitter talk with no let-up from one end of the day to the other. On top of that he's badly shaped, bald-headed, broken winded, bandy-legged and well advanced in the years. He's as hairy as a badger, swarthy as turf mould and poisonous as a wasp. In his favour there is very little," Dan continued, "very little saving the fact that he has his own farm, his own house and from what I can gather he's not short of a shilling."

Having said this, Dan Paddy Andy looked into his whiskey glass which was empty. One of the Corkmen rushed to the bar counter to remedy this while Dan sat scratching his jaw pondering the ins and outs of the case.

"We realise," said the hackney driver, "that we might be expecting too much in asking you to find a woman for this sorry specimen of manhood."

"Patience," said Dan, "and hear me out. For every man in this world there is a suitable woman, only to find her. As luck would have it, I believe I am acquainted with a specimen who might fill the bill."

"But who in God's name would listen to him cronawning all day?" asked the hackney man.

"Who," said Dan, "but someone that won't be listening." He then went on to explain that there was a woman living with her brother in Brosna by the name of Kitty the Whistler. She was so-called because she was never done with whistling, half to herself, half to the world at large. A man would want to be very near her to catch the notes. In and out of bed she would whistle away to her heart's content. When it wasn't a reel she was whistling it was a jig and when it wasn't either it was a slow air, but always almost inaudible except to those with a very keen sense of hearing. She never listened when the brother started to criticise. She only pretended to. He was a cranky sort of a man and he was extremely hard to please. When he started to give under the sister she would whistle away quite happily, nodding the head in agreement with him all the time and now and then between whistles saying: "That's right God knows" or "'Tis true for you to be sure." In time the brother's bitterness was withered away by this constant mollification and although he started most days in a cantankerous fashion he ended them in a tractable enough way.

No matter what was said to her these were her answers. She had become inured over the years to the brother's perverse ways and had developed her own defences.

"She sounds as if she might do," said the eldest of the four farmers, "but would she consent?"

"Would she what?" said Dan. "Wouldn't she climb Carntoohil to get away from the brother and isn't it the highest thought in every woman's head to be the mistress of her own hearth."

The marriage eventually took place and Dan was paid a modest fee. All waited anxiously after the knot was tied to see what way things would work out. Our man continued as before with his cronawning and caterwauling but all he received in reply was the contented whistling of the Brosna woman and she saying every so often: "That's right God knows" or "'Tis true for you to be sure." On top of that she would nod her head in agreement at all times.

As the years passed the cronawning stopped altogether and so did the whistling. As things turned out the pair were very well matched and Dan Paddy Andy's reputation as a matchmaker grew until he eventually became a sort of a last resort for hopeless cases as well as for any other persons be they rich or poor, tall or small, ugly or handsome, fat or thin.

Chapter 21

Although his sympathies could be said to lie with the cause of the Allies, Dan Paddy Andy's attitude towards the Second World War was in line with the general feelings of the vast majority of the Stacks Mountains inhabitants which amounted to simply, "Let them at it and let us out of it."

It is certain that the people of the Stacks were unaware of the systematic annihilation of European Jewry and were blatantly unwilling to consider the other issues at stake because, after all, had not de Valera opted for neutrality and didn't Dev, the undisputed leader of the Irish people, always know what was best for Ireland.

The IRA of the time expressed open support for the Germans but this support was rendered useless by the fact that they were either unwilling or unable to mount any sort of worthwhile offensive against the British regime or undermine the authority of the Irish government which covertly supported its island neighbour. Whatever about the ins and outs of this it is with the wartime disposition of the Stacks Mountains folk that we must concern ourselves.

The general consensus of opinion of the time was that the war ended prematurely. Farm produce was fetching high prices. The average Stacks Mountains farmer was doing very well for himself. The pigs he produced paid handsome profits as did the eggs and oats, potatoes, turnips and farmers' butter. Creamery butter was rationed, two ounces per head per week, but there was no scarcity of lard or dripping. Tea and sugar were also rationed but these were to be had freely on the black market. In fact there was one local black marketeer who boasted that if the war had lasted an extra year he would have paved the roads of North Kerry with £5 notes.

Local belief held that ill-luck followed black marketeers and indeed there were dramatic instances of this. The real money, as far as the Renagown inhabitants were concerned, was in turf production. Nearly all had their own bogs and the difficulty was keeping up with the demand. The war then was regarded as more of a blessing than a misfortune. It brought prosperity without sacrifice and throughout its duration there was no real awareness of the suffering and carnage in Europe and North America. When it ended there was keen disappointment in many quarters and in others no reaction at all.

"The war is over," announced a visiting inspector at Lyreacrompane Creamery one wonderful morning in May 1945.

"Which war is that, sir?" asked a shawled old lady who sat in her asscart waiting to deliver the contents of her solitary milk tank.

Another incident better illustrates the emotions of the ordinary country people. It occurred twenty miles away in mid-Kerry on the same day, a short distance from the village of Milltown. Rumour had it that the war was over but this could not be confirmed. There were few radios and daily newspapers were not always available on the day they were published.

Towards evening a number of friends and neighbours were gathered at a crossroads about two miles outside Milltown. Passers-by were scarce but then a lone cyclist hove into view. He pedalled at a furious pace and was waving what looked like a white flag over his head as he rode.

"Is the war over then?" called out a spokesman for the anxious people at the crossroads.

"Christ, boys, I know nothing about a war," the cyclist threw back. "All I know is that there's white flour in Milltown."

In the Stacks Mountains there were no celebrations and no speeches but it was felt that cigarettes would become more plentiful and that the rationing would be lifted. There was, it could be said, a sense of relief without jubilation. The end of the war, alas for the people of the Stacks, was the signal for the beginning of the mass emigration which at its peak saw 50,000 people (three out of five of its young people) leave Ireland every year. There was to be no outcry. It was the final solution for the people of rural Ireland. It was taken absolutely for granted. For most exiles, although heart-breaking, it was escape from the stifling moral climate. Others, many of them intellectuals, followed George Moore's advice: "Ireland is a fatal disease from which it is the plain duty of every Irishman to disassociate himself." Joyce put it somewhat differently in his *Portrait of the Artist as a Young Man*. Said he, "When the soul of a man is born in this country, there are nets flung out to hold it back from flight. You talk to me of nationality, language and religion. I shall try to fly those nets."

There were many who saw Ireland's rôle in the war as cynical and dastardly, saw the Irish as a nation willing to accept the sacrifices of others but unwilling to give anything in return. These conveniently forgot the thousands of volunteer Irish who died fighting on the side of the Allies.

Nicholas Monserrat in his immortal novel *The Cruel Sea* devotes two blistering pages to castigating Ireland for the passsive rôle it played and the Northern poet Louis Mac Neice conveyed a passionate sense of outrage in his poem "Neutrality": "to the west of your own shores the mackerel/ Are fat — on the flesh of your kin."

There were many other influential voices urging Ireland to join the Allies but de Valera remained unmoved.

Unquestionably the sympathy of the vast majority of the Irish people leaned towards the British; but always underneath was the reality that the vast majority could never endorse physical support to a power which, until a generation before, had subjected Ireland to centuries of oppression.

The Stacks Mountains people were truly thankful to the war and even more thankful for having been kept out of it. Most of them had long been in the habit of doing nothing for themselves, of being content to silently suffer want and deprivation until the Second World War lifted them out of the rut. Dan Paddy Andy was an exception. He lifted himself up in protest of his own accord and confronted the world. He made his own demands upon this world and knew personal fulfilment as well as bringing fulfilment to the backward, the lonely, the outcast and the inarticulate wretches who might otherwise have been doomed to unwanted celibacy till the end of their days.

Chapter 22

In 1941 the Irish Army came to Lyreacrompane. They numbered several hundred and in the summer evenings they bathed and swam in the sparkling waters of the Smearla. Dan's dancehall stood near the Cross of Renagown, less than 200 yards from where the valley began. Not so the river itself, for one would have to travel to the slopes of the distant Glanrudderies to find its beginnings.

There are many in Lyreacrompane who still say that Dan Paddy Andy made money out of the soldiers. Certainly they filled his dancehall on Sunday nights and holiday nights, but if he made money itself the soldiers also made money out of Dan and the other farmers of Renagown.

The Emergency Men, as they were sometimes called, were frugally but adequately fed. Never, however, were they overfed, so to supplement their diets and their incomes they worked during off-duty periods for farmers mostly in the bogs and meadows. Their war then was against the formidable moorland and the deep peat deposits of Renagown which had to be excavated with slean and pike. Most lived under canvas but there were two wooden huts, one which was used as a recreational centre and the other as a mess and bar. In the winter when the turf was harvested most returned to Ballymullen Barracks in Tralee or to Cork and Limerick to await the spring. A small detachment remained on in Renagown throughout the winter months.

Dan told us that he sometimes knew when a fake coin was being passed off on him but that for the sake of peace and friendly relations he kept his mouth shut. Apparently a favourite pastime among the less disciplined members of the army, after having failed to gain admission, was to shower fist-sized stones and black cadhrawns on top of the corrugated iron roof of the dancehall. When this was done in concert the noise resembled thunder. Remember that these were drilled men who knew how to extract maximum advantage from such situations. When Dan Paddy Andy and a few friends went to investigate, the culprits had faded into the dun-dark landscape, silently skirting dangerous bogholes and trenches where older less fit men might end up if they risked pursuit.

Inside the hall the noise was simply unendurable. Women would come screaming out the doorway with their fingers thrust into their ears demanding their money back. Dan endured this for a period and finally complained to the officers in charge. His complaint had the desired effect for a while, but only for a while. He then appointed a look-out man and paid him in advance at the look-out man's insistence. If anything there was an intensification of the barrage so that Dan was driven to his wit's end and considered the permanet closure of the hall.

Never a man to be rebuffed by reverses Dan Paddy Andy hit upon a novel scheme. He commissioned the proprietor of an ancient lorry to deliver a load of turf mould to the rear of the hall. This he spread on the roof to a depth of a foot or so. That night when the younger soldiers started their tatarara they were astonished to hear not a single sound. They redoubled their efforts to no avail. This soon put a stop to the rock-throwing. Then an attempt was made to burn down the hall but a torrential downpour nipped this foul act of arson in the bud.

As World War II reached its climax there was an upswing in the attendances at the dances. Take into account the facts that crossroads and platform dances were no longer as popular as they used to be and that Dan employed highly talented musicians only and the success of the hall is easily explained. The nearest opposition halls of this kind were the Six Crosses hall three miles from Listowel and Headley's Bridge hall between Abbeyfeale and Castleisland.

Joe Sheehy of the Ivy Bridge recalls of the soldiers "that they were a grand bunch and I saw some fierce scraps in that mess and outside of it but never involving more than two soldiers. There were no hard feelings afterwards either."

It was the law of the encampment that under no circumstances was a third party to join in any fight no matter what the outcome was likely to be. The two protagonists fought it out to the finish, always with bare knuckles, until one was unable to get up. When the fight was over the victor always helped the vanquished to his feet and they drank together while they licked their not inconsiderable wounds.

Paying customers from the neighbourhood were always welcome to the mess as long as they behaved themselves. It is also most heartening to relate that those thugs who were banned from Dan Paddy Andy's hall were also unwelcome in the army mess. The soldiers thought a lot of Dan and felt that his feelings might be hurt by their presence.

"The soldiers would spend their last penny on you if you done them a good turn," Joe Sheehy remembers. "They had a great sense of fair play and if you stood a few of them a drink on a Tuesday or a Wednesday night when they were broke they'd make you as drunk as a stick on a Thursday night after they drew their weekly pay."

They harvested thousands of tons of good quality peat both for the army and the surrounding bog owners. They were disciplined workers and they were proud of their skills and their output.

"They left us no legacies," Dan Paddy Andy recalled. "Not one that I remember sired any of our local mares."

Dan was known to the soldiers by the name of "Plenty Cotton".

"Here comes Plenty Cotton," they would whisper respectfully as Dan wended his way from his hall to the mess for the meal which always awaited him. He earned the name from standing at the door of the Renagown hall on summer nights shouting out to all and sundry:

"Come on in lads; plenty cotton here."

This is not to suggest that the girls of the district wore cotton dresses only. A few of the older and sedater dames wore satin frocks but these would be in a minority. The standard apparel was your cotton frock underneath which was a slip, a chemise, a chastity cord (as suggested by the missioners) and a doughty pair of long, sensible bloomers designed to withstand any onslaught which might take place in the heat of the moment when a red-blooded couple found themselves alone in the world with no company save the sedge and rush and no sound save the bleating of the goureen roe or jacksnipe. All the female undergarments were manufactured from flour bags, notably the Sunrise and Pride of the West brands.

There is one man in particular, now living in the city of

Limerick and whose name is Bill Nash. He was then a buck private although he wound up a sergeant. The last time I met him he told me that he has a recurring dream. There he is, a raw recruit, a mere gorsoon as green as the spring shoots in the deep surrounding valleys with his volunteer cap perched jauntily on the side of his close-cropped head. He is standing outside the Renagown hall with a group of his fellows listening to the enchanting music of Tom Doran and dreaming sweet romantic dreams. He sees Dan Paddy Andy O'Sullivan standing at the door jingling silver pieces in his trousers pockets and his voice as clear as though it were direct from that golden yesterday:

"Come on in lads. Plenty cotton here!"

After that he remembers the turfcutting and the footing and the drawing to the road and the everlasting turf dust which reddened his young eyes day in, day out.

Dan had great regard for the soldiers and while they remained in Renagown, in a large dry hillside field known as Gleanndearg, he was always welcome to whatever fare was available in the mess. He dined there regularly and according to eye witnesses had an appetite the equal of any two able-bodied troops, "and remember," said an assistant cook who was often present in the mess, "Dan would be after eating his own dinner at home no more than an hour or two before."

According to Dan Canty, Dan Paddy Andy had an insatiable appetite for food.

"He could put away as much as any two men I ever saw; and talk of a sweet tooth, sure a dozen of buns was only like a rush in a bull's mouth to him when he broke fast on the morning of a cattle fair. He was the only man I ever saw who would dip a bun into a glass of porter and relish it. He'd have his dinner later in some eating house and I swear to you they made no profit out of Dan. He'd eat anything fat or lean. His policy was leave nothing on the table except the ware."

In spite of his extraordinary appetite his weight was only a stone above normal. Also he was physically fitter than most men of his age. Often when no car stopped to offer him a lift he would be obliged to walk all the way home from Castle-island. In the end he would take a lift anywhere whether Killarney, Tralee, Abbeyfeale or Listowel. He preferred to be out and about rather than confined to the hearth like others of his age.

John Donnellan recalls that Dan was brought before the court for having no toilets in the Renagown hall.

"M'anam ón diabhal," said Dan to the judge, "if you was to come with me I'd show you toilets galore. All you have to do if you're caught short is to go out the door of the hall and you have 2,000 acres of toilets."

In spite of the extra earnings and their own weekly wages of 13s. 2d. which was to leap dramatically shortly afterwards to 21s., the soldiers were nearly always chronically short of cash. This militated against trips to Castleisland which was greatly to Dan Paddy Andy's benefit.

About this time too Dan was receiving his usual unfavourable mention from the pulpits of not-too-distant churches. The clergy, misled by mischievous accounts of atrocious goings-on after Sunday afternoon and Sunday night dances warned their flocks against attending the "den of iniquity" at the Cross of Renagown. Not all priests were so gullible and those made no mention whatsoever of the hall no matter what stories reached them from time to time.

But for the fact that his hall was so isolated Dan Paddy Andy might have wound up a millionaire. Petrol too was rationed at the time and the only method of transport for young people was shanks mare. Few had bicycles and those who had were often without tubes or tyres. Still he did a lively trade but only a fraction of what he might have done during the Lenten period when he had no opposition. The hall was situated at Renagown Cross, seven miles from Castleisland, twelve from Tralee and fourteen from Listowel.

Today there is no sign whatsover of this historic building. Not even a vestige of the walls remain. Recently I passed that way on my way home from Tralee. I left the car on a grass margin and sauntered along the narrow road that leads to the valley of Castleisland. A shrouded moon, sickled and pale, looked down on the silver landscape and only the frogs and crickets intruded upon the enchanted silence. I looked to that spot where row after row of tents once stood like giant mushrooms in the aftergrass of the hillside fields and waited for the plaint of a service bugle. No sound came but behind the mist that enshrouded the hills and valleys the melodies of that golden time are still drifting around and around.

It is an easy matter to conjure up the baby faces of the freshly uniformed volunteers as they stood outside the dancehall on a Sunday evening during the first summer after their arrival. Easier still to see them licking their fingers after downing their rations of McConachie's stew, canned in Roscrea from the most venerable beeves that money could buy.

It is impossible, however, to recapture the hazy, lazy atmosphere of the early Forties. Perhaps it is because nobody had more than enough in those days and there were no strikes for the good reason that there were no jobs. It was a different climate altogether. There was little or no crime and it could be argued that the severity of the confessional was partly the cause. In the diocese of Kerry perjury was a reserved sin, that is to say that only the bishop had the authority to forgive such a sin. There is no doubt whatsoever but that diocesan laws were designed to complement civil laws and in this they succeeded.

The soldiers were seldom or ever short of the threepenny piece which was the entrance fee to the Renagown hall. These were good years for Dan and he was never short of money. His sons worked in the bogs futting and re-futting the drying sods. Later when Dan's fortunes receded they would all emigrate to America. By this time the army had long gone from Renagown. The population was drastically reduced and nine-tenths of the employable youth had vanished overseas and the once cultivated plots surrendered again to the encroaching moorland.

Chapter 23

In the course of compiling these chapters I interviewed several couples who had been originally brought together by Dan and who were, I am happy to be able to report, well pleased with themselves after long terms of marriage. Not one of the blessed pairs had ever laid eyes on each other until Dan arranged for them to meet and take stock of each other for the first time. Dan, therefore, was soley responsible for the marriages.

"I often pray for Dan Paddy Andy," said Noranne Hickey of Renagown. "I never saw nor met with Mickey until Dan went matchmaking for him."

The Hickeys, Mickey and Noranne, now hale and hearty in their spotless home near the Cross of Renagown, could well be described as a typical Dan Paddy Andy pairing.

"We have thirty-eight years of marriage behind us," Noranne boasted, "and every one of those years were good. We saw hard times and good, the same as our friends and neighbours, but we were always content and happy and we always had the grace of God."

As for her husband Mickey he is absolutely convinced that he would never have found a partner but for the good offices of Dan Paddy Andy, who also happened to be his mother's first cousin.

Mickey was in his twenty-eighth year when he made it known to Dan that the single way of life was no longer sufficient for him. Renagown was considered to be an out of the way place with little attraction for young women, so that Dan's work was cut out for him. He racked his brains as was his wont until from the back of his mind he resurrected a tale he had been told about a bright young miss working in the town of Castleisland. Apparently this independent-minded lassie had defied her father and turned down the suitor which he would have her wed. At the time Noranne was working as a domestic servant at Mary Julia O'Grady's, now Tom McCarthy's, of Castleisland when the first suggestion of marriage was put to her.

She pointed out to her father that his choice was not her choice, that she would marry for love and not for property or status. Her father was too fond of her to press her into a marriage she did not want and when Dan Paddy Andy approached her with an account of Mickey Hickey she listened eagerly to all he had to say and indicated that a meeting with this shy young man from Renagown might not be amiss. Duly they met, in Dan's presence of course, and took to each other at once. Dan then paid a visit to Noranne's father at his abode in Knockreagh, Scartaglin, near Castleisland to discuss a date and a dowry.

At the time Noranne was twenty-five years of age. In rural districts this was regarded as a young age for a marrying couple. More often than not the bride and groom would be in their thirties and frequently in their forties. An unwritten farm law of the period was the cause. Before a girl could marry into a country household the way had to be made clear. This would involve marrying off any daughter or daughters of the house and if necessary finding dowries for them which would be commensurate with the value of the farms into which they might be marrying. Failing this, passage money to America would be expected. It also involved providing for a younger son or sons who would be obliged to leave the house and it also included providing for the old couple who nearly always remained on in the house in a room specially set aside for them.

A solicitor would draw up an agreement which would protect the interests of the old couple. There would be a guarantee of access to the hearth and a place beside the hearth, a guarantee of a stipulated number of potato drills, vegetables, flitches of bacon, pints of milk, eggs, etc. and often a small percentage of the monthly creamery cheque to supplement their old age pensions. The incoming woman, alas, did not always honour the agreement and eventually most old couples bought small houses or rented rooms in the nearest town or insisted that the young couples build their own homes.

Not long before the marriage of Mickey Hickey and Noranne Flynn, Dan Paddy Andy brought all the interested parties together at Mary Julia O'Grady's which also happened to be a public house. A dowry of £85 was handed over to

Mickey Hickey. The stock on his farm at the time consisted of four milch cows, a pony and a bawnie calf. Bawnie or white calves were not held in high regard. In fact they have disappeared altogether from the rural scene. Most bawnies were killed when they were calves. The skin was ideal for the making of bodhrawns. Many people of the time believed that bawnies brought bad luck, that they were descended from fairy cattle and ran with the fairy herds at night when Christians were in their beds and the moon reigned over the world.

The real fault in white cattle, of course, was that they suffered from photosensitisation in the hotter summers. They were allergic to sun. In the winter the rain seriously affected them. The hide was light and there was lack of pigmentation. They were, quite simply, poor survivors although with care and luck they were capable of matching any other colour of cattle. They were also tempermentally unpredictable and bawnie cows were known to attack human beings without provocation. Many bawnie heifers, because of certain physical deficiencies, were unable to play host to the bull.

Mickey and Noranne Hickey were married on 8 November 1945. In Europe about the same time the Nuremberg trials of German war criminals opened. In April of the same year Franklin Delano Roosevelt, president of the USA died in his bed. Vice-president Harry Truman took over and saw the war to a successful conclusion. The ill-starred Mussolini was captured by Italian partisans and executed without the formality of a trial. The first atomic bombs were dropped on Hiroshima and Nagasaki and in the Flynn home in Scartaglin a lone musician, Tom Sullivan of the same address, supplied the music for the wedding reception of Noranne and Mickey Hickey with a single key melodeon.

Sonny Nolan of Castleisland provided the taxi service to and from the church. His fee on the occasion was the princely sum of 9s. Noranne Hickey recalls that there were a dozen guests and that it was an unforgettable occasion with no scarcity of drink, food or music.

According to Mickey Hickey, Dan Paddy Andy's fee was a blueback (a £10 note) but because of the relationship between Mickey's mother and Dan this was reduced to a fiver.

The Hickeys had one daughter, now happily married in Tralee with three children of her own. Although a fee for this match was only a £5 note Dan considered himself well paid. There was little or no travel involved. Mickey Hickey was a near neighbour and Scartaglin was only a few miles from Castleisland, a town which Dan was in the habit of frequenting regularly. Of course, he was no stranger to Killarney, Tralee, Listowel and Abbeyfeale, where he conducted business in the snugs of numerous public houses, but Castleisland remained his favourite haunt to the end of his days.

Chapter 24

Dan Paddy Andy had six children, five boys and one girl. Two of the boys succumbed to the plague of scarlet fever which swept the country in the early Forties. It was widely believed at the time, although never verified, that this murderous fever was caused by the decay of corpses in the battlefields and concentration camps of Hitler's Europe. True or not one thing is absolutely certain and that is that the war period brought with it diseases and fevers on an unprecedented scale.

In the town of Castleisland people still talk about the day Dan Paddy Andy's children were buried. Dan was a great favourite in the town and the hearts of the townspeople went out to him in his grief.

Chris Jer Davy Nolan, who presently farms at Renagown, recalls Dan's agony after the death of his two sons.

"He'd give the night around the outside of the house crying and sobbing, and that was every night for months after they were buried. He never got over their loss, not until the day he died."

Eventually Dan's other sons Patsy, Jimmy and Johnny emigrated to America. They had been preceded by his only daughter Mary. Dan's wife, who hailed originally from Cearcar in Scartaglin, followed her children to America after Dan's death in 1966. She died and was buried there a few years ago.

After the loss of his sons Dan Paddy Andy mourned for a long period. He closed his dancehall, abandoned the trade of matchmaking and never left his farm except to go to mass.

He might never have returned to the trade of matchmaking but for an unexpected challenge. A young curate in a parish in the west of Kerry paid a visit to Dan one night during the spring following the winter which saw the burial of his sons.

There was a most ungainly fellow in his parish who found it impossible to make out a wife. For years the priest had tried in vain to find a wife for him and was on the point of abandoning hope when he chanced to hear of Dan Paddy

Andy. As well as being rough, the poor fellow was shy but he managed, in desperation, to pluck up sufficient courage to tell his tale to the curate.

Dan Paddy Andy explained to the cleric that he had given up matchmaking but he recommended another man in Abbeyfeale who used to dabble a little in the marriage business. The curate, however, pressed his case and brought in his man who had been seated all the time in the back seat of the curate's Baby-Ford. The reason he sat in the back, and sideways at that, was that he was too big and too ungainly for the front seat. Dan looked at him and shook his head.

"You'll never get a woman for him," Dan said.

"Ah!" said the curate, "that's a shame for with all his awkwardness he's a gentle sort of a fellow and can play the fiddle."

"If he played the organ and the piano together," said Dan, "he'll never get a woman. He's too thick and too weighty and too ugly. Sure he's more like a gorilla than a man."

"I thought," said the curate, "that nothing was beyond Dan Paddy Andy, but I'm afraid I was wrong, for the great Dan Paddy Andy is only the same as ourselves."

So saying he swept his man before him to the door. His ruse worked for the remark riled Dan.

"Toughen," said Dan, "toughen a tamall."

The curate halted his man and returned to the fireplace, where he had been standing. Dan excused himself and went up to the Room. In a minute he was back with a fiddle and a bow.

"Now," said Dan, "here's a fiddle. Let's see what he'll knock out of it."

He handed over the fiddle and bow and straightaway the man from the west began to play. There was no tune to his music and there was no rhythm. Such a dreadful charivari had never before been heard in Renagown. Outside in the night cats began to answer. Dan snatched the instrument from the man's hands.

"He can drive a fiddle alright," said Dan, "but he can't play a fiddle."

"Is there anything at all to be done for the poor fellow?" the curate asked.

"He's in luck," Dan confided. "Beyond in Tubbernanoon there is a lady who draws the blind pension, the same as I do. She's not gone altogether in the sight but there isn't enough vision for her to get a right gander at your man. In addition, she's tone-deaf and wouldn't know a hornpipe from a foxtrot. As I recall, she's still single and might, if she was asked in the right way, take her place by this outsize fostook in front of an altar."

The curate pumped Dan's hand in thanks.

"Handshakes," said Dan, "won't buy butter."

The curate got the message and a satisfactory agreement was reached. The couple were married the first Saturday of the following September and they lived happily ever after. "Which is more," said Dan, "than can be said for the million-aires of America who think so little of marriage that they throw it to one side whenever it suits them."

Chapter 25

In 1946, a year after the end of World War II, faint rays of hope began to penetrate the gloom which hung over war-ravished Europe. A peace conference was held in Paris which culminated in numerous successful treaties. The Security Council and General Assembly of the UN met for the first time and ten leading Nazi war criminals were hanged. Perversely, however, no punishment of any kind was meted out to the many profiteers who became millionaires at the expense of millions of war dead.

True that in the following year New York playwright Arthur Miller in his searing play *All My Sons* brought this form of corruption to the fore when he highlighted the rise and fall of a manufacturer of defective war materials. Otherwise little or nothing was done to bring these and other war criminals from the civilian scene to justice.

In 1946 another form of corruption attempted to rear its ugly head in the Stacks Mountains. It was Dan Paddy Andy O'Sullivan who, single-handed, attempted to nip this rare perversion in the bud — with no thanks from the clergy who had hounded him for so long.

It was a sultry afternoon in July. Dan had just returned from the meadow where he had cocked the last of his hay. He had hardly seated himself with his sons to a fine meal of bacon, cabbage and floury new spuds when a resounding knock came to the door.

Kate O'Brien called, "Come in, whoever it is," and straightaway the latch was lifted.

Enter two powerfully built, gnarly men in their thirties. Without enquiring whether they were fasting or otherwise, which was the custom of Renagown people, Kate handed each a plate of edibles and bade them to be seated on two sugawns near the hearth. There they masticated with great relish and abandon and were aided in their noisy gulps and swallows by two brimming pannies of prime buttermilk.

When the meal was over they asked Dan if they might have a word with him in private. Kate O'Brien was quick to take the hint and without more ado went out of doors with her flock and postponed the washing and drying of the ware until the visitors would have concluded their business.

"Well boys!" Dan opened, "and what is it that I can do for ye?"

The visitors explained that they were brothers from the banks of Brick River, the Feale's third largest tributary after the Gale and Smearla. It appeared that their aged mother and father had died the previous winter within weeks of each other and that the small farm on which the four had managed to survive until then had been willed to the two.

It was a rushy holding which was always tested to the utmost, year after year, to sustain the eight milch cows which cropped it. The pair had fought a long, arduous mixed battle against rush and water and had somehow managed to keep their heads above the latter.

Of money they had but little. However, there was enough to handsomely compensate Dan for any endeavours that would be made by him to see them settled in marriage. Dan told his visitors that he foresaw no problems and expressed some surprise that such well-made, presentable fellows had not been waylaid by marriageable females before this. Each had the humility to bend his head in modesty before explaining their dilemma in more detail.

"You see," said the older, "it isn't two women we want at all. One will do the two of us grand."

Dan could scarcely believe his ears.

"You see, sir," said the younger brother uncouthly, "whilst we might barely manage to feed and dress one there is no way we could support two."

Dan bridled. To be called "sir" was nothing less than a glaring example of hypocrisy. The older brother took up where the younger had left off.

"We are aisy," said he with a grin, "which of us goes to the railings with her once as the two of us has the same claim on her after."

Dan marvelled at their insolence but decided to play the game to the close.

"What about children?" he asked. "Won't half of the craturs be illegitimate?"

"Oh, there's no danger of that," the older brother assured

him, "because, supposing the brood has different sires itself, they will all be baptised and christened as the legal offspring of which ever one of us goes to the altar."

"And pray," asked Dan, "which one of you will that be?"

"We'll toss a coin for that," said the younger brother, "and maybe after you make out a woman for us you might be good enough to throw the coin in the air yourself."

"Have you consulted your parish priest about this?" Dan asked.

"What would we want to go and do a foolish thing like that for?" said the older brother. "What he won't know won't trouble him."

"Now," said Dan, "I'll tell ye one thing and one thing alone and this is it. If ye're not gone out of here by the count of three, there will be blood spilt."

"If there will," said the brothers of one accord, "it won't be our blood." With that they flexed their mighty muscles and assumed the poses of boxers. Said the elder, "Hand us over our expenses now like a good man or we'll make orphans of your children."

"Expenses!" Dan echoed in amazement.

"That's right," said the younger brother. "We have wasted a half day in coming here and before we leave we'll be wanting a fair day's pay between the two of us."

Dan smiled before he spoke again.

"Shove in here a bit closer," said he, "until I make my position clear on this matter." Warily the brothers shoved nearer Dan until they were close enough. He then seized each by an ear and banged their heads together. They staggered dizzily around the kitchen until Dan came to their aid with two well-aimed kicks on their respective posteriors which dispatched them in the direction of the door and the outside world. There they rambled in utter confusion for several minutes before coming to their senses, after which Dan seized each by the scruff of the neck and ran them as far as the Cross of Renagown where he implanted two more kicks which speeded their departure forever from the bailiwick of Dan Paddy Andy.

The odd thing was that they succeeded in locating the kind of woman they wanted without Dan's help. She married one but played the rôle of wife to two. At the time of writing she lives widowed with her daughter, one of many which resulted from this strange relationship.

Chapter 26

Often over a drink when he had an attentive audience Dan Paddy Andy would boast that he had increased the population of Ireland by over 2,000 souls. Of the 400 marriages which he arranged there were approximately fifty childless for the simple reason that the couples were too old when they hit the tick for the first time. In cases like these where the bloom had vanished, constant endeavour as Dan called it was of little use although it paid off occasionally. Success at this late stage was often attributed to novenas and other forms of prayer. Dan disagreed although he was a great believer in prayer.

"Prayer is good," he would say, "and endeavour is good but an active young damsel is the best guarantee of all. Better still if she has an active young man."

Often when it was discovered that no issue would be forthcoming after years of honest endeavour on the part of the male of the pairing it was not uncommon for husband and wife to sit down and have a heart to heart talk concerning their plight. I heard Dan recall at least two instances where it was agreed that the wife should fare forth on her own to the Pattern of Ballybunion on 15 August, there to make herself available to a young, vigorous and lusty rustic, by no means for the pleasure of the ravishment involved but solely to return home, as it were, with better prospects of producing progeny. Dan mentioned others who visited the same Pattern and the Patterns of Knocknagoshel and Bally-heigue (wherever they might be the least known) and who failed altogether to succeed in their primary objectives. He mentioned another lady well past her prime who journeyed here, there and everywhere for seven years until she was blossomed to the tune of two and fifty years and had abandoned all hope when out of the blue one night in the port of Fenit she accomplished her mission and in the course of time produced for her delighted husband a bouncing baby boy.

The Fair of Puck, of course, was the last resort of such

cases. As Dan put it in his own inimitable way, "There was never a misser out of Puck."

"'Tis hard to have to send a woman out to Puck and places like that and 'tis hard to say whether 'tis right or wrong but right or wrong the child is blameless and it will have love and security and that's all any child wants."

Dan maintained that the 350 productive marriages had an average of six children to each. Hence his claim that he was the cause of the huge increase in the population. Truth to tell it is highly unlikely that the marriages would have taken place but for his intercession. Many of them would, no doubt, but the vast majority of the people he joined together were neither articulate enough nor presumptious enough to act on their own.

One morning Dan was in receipt of a solicitor's letter on behalf of a client who claimed that he had been duped. Apparently the woman provided for him by Dan was a good deal older than Dan said and would not be in a position to give birth to a child. Rather than spend hard-earned money engaging another solicitor Dan went to the plaintiff with a view to talking some sense into him.

"All he wanted at first was law," Dan recalled, "but when I told him what the full cost of the law might be he wasn't long drawing on his reins." Dan later spent a whole night drinking with him and gave him some sound advice. Not too long after Dan's visit a little with three months to be exact, news came that a miracle of some kind had been performed and that the woman was expecting a baby. There were many who tried to take the credit for this unexpected happening. The curate put it down to a novena which he had recommended when first the couple were joined together. A reverend mother who was distantly related to the woman put it down to her own prayers, while the dispensary doctor put it down to a tonic which he had prescribed to supplement certain mineral deficiencies. There was no credit whatsoever given to the father of the child and the injustice of this greatly annoyed him. When it came to the christening there was great rejoicing.

"You can thank my prayers," one party said.

"You can put it down to my novena," another party announced.

"No one need tell me what to put it down to," said the father, "for I know well 'twas the counsel given to me by Dan Paddy Andy."

"Don't leave the bed," Dan had said, "until you haven't the strength to lace your shoes."

This is all to show what a very wise, sage and thoughtful individual was Dan Paddy Andy O'Sullivan.

"Give me a fair slip and a long course," Dan once confided to me, "and there's no hare I won't turn."

Chapter 27

If the clergy were silent about matchmaking some of Dan's enemies were not.

"Why should he be getting two pensions, one blind and one old IRA," they asked, "when he has the income from his farm, from his dancehall and from his matchmaking?"

It was rumoured around this time that Dan had earned a hundred pounds from a single match. Dan never denied this. In fact he related the story to us one night in Teddy O'Connor's public house in Killarney.

It appeared that Dan was approached by a strapping man in his late twenties who sought the hand of a well-built, healthy farmer's daughter, an only child, who lived no more than a stone's throw from his own dwellinghouse.

On previous occasions he had made his intentions clear and the girl herself had seemed responsive enough, but only provided her father gave his blessing to the bond. This the old man stoutly refused to do, opting instead for a small, ancient, wizened farmer who also lived within easy access of the girl and whose many verdant acres were separated by no more than a tiny rivulet from the even more verdant acres of the only daughter.

When the young man came to Dan Paddy Andy and explained his case the venerable matchmaker scratched his head and confessed that he was somewhat mystified. The young man in question had a thriving place with healthy cows and a fine house. He was also an only son with money to burn. He struck Dan, however, in the absence of evidence to the contrary, as a suanach, that is to say a man not in possession of the equipment to put the human seal on a marriage. When Dan pointed out his suspicions the young man denied the charge hotly. When asked by Dan if he would be willing to submit himself for medical inspection he announced that he was agreeable.

The pair went to Listowel where Dan's physician Dr Johnny Walsh resided. Dr Johnny assured Dan after inspection that his candidate was as fine a specimen of manhood as he had ever come across.

"That," said Dan to the doctor, "is the best piece of news I've heard in many a long day for there will be a mighty fee following this if all goes well."

"Now," said Dan to his young client, "we must take ourselves to a photographer."

When the young man asked for what reason, Dan informed him that it was to allay any fears the father of his choice might have regarding his masculinity. After a good deal of persuasion he allowed himself to be photographed in the nude. As soon as prints were available Dan made tracks for the house in question where he cornered the father of the girl. When they found themselves alone Dan produced the photograph and handed it to the old man, who examined it hastily, nodded his head and handed it back.

"Now are you satisfied?" said Dan.

"Satisfied over what?" the old man asked.

"Satisfied," said Dan triumphantly, "that this man has all his faculties."

"I never doubted it," said the old man.

"Then tell me," Dan asked exasperatedly, "why you won't allow your daughter to marry him?"

"I'll tell you," said the old man, "and I won't put a tooth in it. My objection to this man is that he cannot kick a football with his right leg."

"What's wrong with a ciotóg?" Dan asked.

A ciotóg is still the common name in North Kerry for a left-legged person and generally speaking a ciotóg would be regarded as having more power in his left leg than the orthodox footballer would have in his right. In many football teams, in fact, it is to the ciotóg the kicking of penalties is delegated. Such is the force of the kick that even when the ball is blocked by the goalkeeper he never manages to quite hold on to it thereby giving the other forwards a chance to finish the ball to the net. However, it is more or less accepted that a ciotóg is rarely as accurate as the orthodox kicker but it is also accepted that the extra force and distance adequately compensates for this. Dan relayed these views to the father of the girl, but that worthy was having none of it.

"Have you anything else against him?" Dan asked.

"No," the father answered, "there is nothing else."

"And you won't change your mind?" Dan entreated.

"I can't change it now," was the answer, "when she's all but given to the man next door."

"'Tis a riddle to me," said Dan angrily, "this business of right and left legs, for if that oul' man had as many more legs they wouldn't make up for what he's missing."

"Not so," said the old man, "for if this young man of yours was to seed my daughter with sons and if they were to play football they might not be blessed with the use of two legs and as a result they would find it hard to get on the Kerry team, for don't everyone know that you must be able to kick with the two legs if you want to wear the green and gold."

This was the sort of forthright answer Dan Paddy Andy needed. He went to his client and ordered him to go into training, instructing him to practise his right leg till it was as good as his left. The young man practised night and day and after a space of three months he acquired maximum proficiency.

At the next football game in which the young man was engaged the father of his heart's delight was amongst the attendance.

The old man's pleasure knew no bounds when he saw the distance and height of the young farmer's kicking with left and right legs. He slapped him on the back when the game was over and invited him forthwith to the nearest public house where Dan Paddy Andy also happened to be imbibing at the time. Drinks were called for and a happy evening followed.

Dan was paid a record fee for this classic example of matchmaking and was also paid other subventions down the years in lieu of a baker's dozen of lively sons and daughters who appeared regularly to the delight of their ageing grandfather. The young pair I am happy to say lived happily ever after. Alas not one of the several sons could kick a ball with the right leg, which goes to show that breeding will always out no matter how hard one practises to curtail it.

Immediately after the marriage Dan Paddy Andy set out for the house of the poor old fellow who had been spurned at the last moment by his young neighbour. Dan pointed out the high mortality rate among old men who married young

119

women and after a short while convinced him that what he needed was a woman nearer his own age who wouldn't knock as much taspy out of him as a younger bedmate.

By pure accident Dan Paddy Andy happened to have such a woman among his many hopefuls. He was paid the usual fee when the marriage took place, but when a baby boy appeared on the scene and Dan visited the parents for the extra £10 which had been guaranteed in the event of such a blessing it was proudly pointed out to him by the ageing father that, while Dan was certainly entitled to the credit for bringing the pair together, the arrival of the first-born was purely as a result of their own endeavours.

Chapter 28

Dan Paddy Andy's mother was a Geaney from Raemore, a wild but lovely countryside between Renagown Cross and the town of Tralee and Dan was as familiar with Raemore as he was with Lyreacrompane. In was in Raemore that Maurice Moore was tragically murdered in 1958, and it was upon this terrible incident that I based my play *The Field* which was produced at Dublin's Olympia Theatre in 1965.

The crime rate in the Stacks Mountains was insignificant during the lifetime of Dan Paddy Andy. The exception was this murder.

Dan was a good man to make up a difference between neighbours. He never waited to be sent for. He always took the initiative himself, saying there was only one place apart from hell into which he would not venture, that being the dock in a court of law. He was quick to sense bad blood between neighbours and was quick off his mark to prevent a quarrel from developing into something worse. He was shocked, for instance, by the murder of Maurice Moore and it wasn't easy to shock Dan Paddy Andy.

News of illicit pregnancies, elopements, infidelities, love affairs and what-have-you never drew a word of condemnation out of him. At the very most his comment would consist of a shake of the head. He was too well aware of the absurdity of human folly to be taken aback by it. He never had the hard word when news of some sexual transgression came his way, but he was truly aghast when word reached him that Maurice Moore had been murdered. In time the tragedy took a back seat in Raemore and in Lyreacrompane but it was always to the forefront with Dan. A few weeks after the murder I called to see him. He shook his great head.

"This is one business that cannot be fixed or settled," he said solemnly; "there is no shake hands at the end of this. The water in the bogholes will curdle before this is blown away."

He seemed to be truly ashamed of the fact that the crime had taken place in his own bailiwick. It was his love of all living things that led to his reaction in this instance. Dan had never to be reminded that life was God's greatest gift. It was the crowning belief of his life.

"M'anam ón diabhal," Dan would say, "isn't a row a noble thing. A row is the only vent the poor tormented mind has. The couple that goes a long time without a row has seen the back of love but for all that the seed of one row should not be saved to grow another. Let rows be natural and no harm will be done."

Local people in the know still maintain authoritatively that the so-called murder was simply a beating which misfired. The murder set out to chastise rather than kill. The bother was that the victim was physically a much weaker person. Police investigations on the most comprehensive scale failed to find out the murderer and yet his name was on everybody's lips. What happened was that the locals closed ranks when high-ranking members of the Garda Síochána took over the investigation. The quiet and previously unknown hinterland was subject to too-intense publicity and excessive investigation. The natives responded by minding their own business. In their eyes it was a tragic accident rather than a wilful murder. The ensuing publicity and ultimate isolation of the suspect were punishment enough.

I remember visiting the scene of the murder with a friend, Michael Wale, who worked for the *Daily Express*. It was a Sunday afternoon in the early spring and there was a carnival atmosphere around a certain house which was under surveillance by the Garda Síochána.

Michael Wale and I succeeded in gaining access to the house during a diversion. I will never forget the poor huddled figure by the fire. He was the only suspect in the case and, although nothing could be proved against him, he was watched day and night. He remembered me from my youth in nearby Renagown and we spoke for a while.

Nothing, however, could dispel the intolerable air of gloom which hung about the place. Although the suspect was never brought to trial, his sentence was far more savage than any a court of law might impose on him. No matter where he went he was under constant surveillance by the authorities.

Worse still, wherever he went in town or village up to the time of his death he would be pointed out surreptitiously as the man who stood accused. In addition, he was hounded by reporters and it is no wonder that he finally cracked. He died before his time from a succession of heart attacks.

Chapter 29

Let us look now at one of the more painful aspects of Dan's career as a matchmaker. He would always maintain that only half of his customers had paid him in full. After they were successfully settled down the rest would find loopholes in the original bargain.

Dan was often forced to neglect his farm in order to travel long journeys and the very least he was entitled to in return was his expenses. In the 1940's when he was in his heyday his charge was a £1 per milch cow and corresponding sums for other stock. There were separate charges for labourers and tradesmen and if an aspiring candidate lived near enough to Dan Paddy Andy's holdings he could pay his fee by coring, that is to say he could work off his debts on Dan's farm.

Dan kept eight to ten cows and a horse and added to the income from his monthly creamery contribution by selling horse rails of turf in Tralee and Castleisland. He rarely came to Listowel or Abbeyfeale because the distances were too far and because both towns have numerous bogs within their own parish districts; and it was difficult to compete with local suppliers who would have but a mere mile or two to travel against Dan Paddy Andy's thirteen and twenty respectively.

There were times when Dan imposed no charge for his services. I remember we were sitting by the fire one evening when Jule Seán Sheehy drew down the name of an aged and benighted bachelor who hadn't an acre of land or a brown penny to his name. He had a tidy little cottage however, and he was not afraid of a day's work.

"Wisha, Dan," said Jule Seán as he handed him a cup of tea, "wouldn't you work your best endeavours some day soon and find a partner for that poor oul' aingisheoir?"

Jule Seán had no need to say more or to remind Dan thereafter.

"I'll make out some lady for him alright," Dan would promise and the promise was kept.

In those days Dan found it difficult to make ends meet. Everybody else was in the same boat and apart from professional people, traders and big farmers, very few country people had cash reserves of any consequence.

The tragedy about Dan's untimely death, he was only sixty-six, was that he was never as well off as he was before he died. He had money to spare and ample pensions. He had sold his farm to the Land Commission for a better than average price. The more fertile of his fields were divided among local farmers while the boggier area was used for forestry.

In the Forties and Fifties, Dan's average fee was £20. If there were other expenses involved, such as food and travel, these would always be paid for by the male contractor.

Paddy Doran's charges to Dan were minimal because Paddy maintained that a day in Dan's company was the best entertainment for which a man could wish. Paddy was always paid, however. Dan would insist upon this at the start of the proceedings. Paddy, who lives in Carrigcannon in Lyreacrompane, has countless tales to tell about Dan.

Paddy Doran describes how one morning he drove Dan to Listowel to purchase a trap. Dan knocked at the auctioneer's door and addressed the man's wife as follows:

"Good morning, sir. You're a fine-looking man, God bless you."

Later when the trap was bought Dan, accompanied by Paddy, went to see Fred Mann the jeweller in the Small Square. The shop was closed so Dan knocked upon the door. Receiving no reply he called out: "Are you alive or dead, Mann? Are you alive or dead?"

After several minutes Mann appeared, sleepy-eyed and haggard.

Dan drew off his glasses.

"Will you repair these for me like a good man, Mann?" Dan said. Mann replied that he did not repair glasses.

"In that case," said Dan, "you might as well be dead."

Dan would keep a meticulous account of a day's journey on behalf of his client. Every expense was jotted down and if these were not paid by the end of the day Dan merely held on to the fiver deposit which he always demanded at the beginning of any bargain.

As soon as the knot was tied the balance of the money

was handed over to Dan, although there were many who tried to opt out of the bargain. In spite of the amounts he earned Dan was nearly always short of money. No shame this as it was a national disease at the time. Paddy Doran will readily state that Dan lost more than he gained at the business of matchmaking. He liked good food and he was a decent man in a public house so that there was little, if any, profit at the end of the proceedings.

The making of certain matches, however, was far more complicated than simply agreeing upon a certain sum and closing the deal at that. There were numerous conditions and in certain cases these were extremely complicated.

Let us look at a classical example of the more difficult type of match. In May of 1945 Dan introduced a girl from Lixnaw in North Kerry to a farmer from the east of Killarney. The Lixnaw girl was in her late thirties and her prospective husband was just turned forty. The entire business took up three whole days and several nights of Dan's time. It also involved considerable expense.

Dan's fee was a modest £20. Hardly worth his while you might say. There were, however, some extra advantages if things turned out the right way. There was a promise, for instance, of an extra £20 if there was a son born to the couple. There might also be a promise of another £5 for a second son or daughter.

These clauses were more to the advantage of the client than they were to Dan. Dan would have little to gain if there were no children so naturally it would be in his best interests to ensure that the female of the partnership came from stock that was noted for its fertility. This was especially important where the woman was coming to the end of her child-bearing years. He would see to it that she came from a large family and it would also be a help if she had married sisters who had large families. The husband-to-be was, therefore, more or less in the hands of the matchmaker regarding the number of offspring, if any, he was likely to father. This may seem harsh or commercial to some but the reality of the situation was that it was part and parcel of farm life at the time in that part of the world.

The painful aspect to which I referred earlier was that many farmers refused to fork up the extra money when a child appeared. Certainly in the case of the Killarney farmer there wasn't a single penny of the promised £20 forthcoming when the first son appeared. Although there was no legal contract, the Lixnaw girl was mortified by her husband's refusal to pay. However, she paid Dan in dribs and drabs down the years unknown to her husband.

In most cases the type of farmer who insisted upon these clauses was a busy, hardworking fellow whose life was dominated by cattle and crops and the general making of money. He wouldn't have time to make out a girl himself, particularly if he came from an out-of-the-way district where there were no women. Also it was usually late in life, the early forties at least, before he succeeded to the farm. To him the services of a matchmaker were indispensable, so he insured himself against lack of offspring by introducing the condition about payment for the first son, second son, daughter etc. Normally Dan would expect a fee of up to £50 from a big farmer but this would be where there were no conditions attached.

In many cases the farmers were delighted to pay out after the arrival of a son. Others, mean, ungrateful and dishonourable, would renege on their promises although the promised amount might mean nothing whatsoever to them. It was just that they were naturally tight-fisted.

In these cases there was no redress for Dan except alone the wife died and the farmer sought a second partner. When Dan was told by a friend at the thirteenth of May cattle fair in Listowel that a certain farmer from Ballyheigue was searching the fair for him, Dan was mightily pleased as he thought the farmer sought him out to pay him £10 which was overdue for several years since the birth of a son. When he eventually met the farmer at a public house in the Square of Listowel there was no mention of money.

"How's the missus?" Dan asked after a while thinking it might jolt the scoundrel's memory into forking up the money.

"We delivered the poor creature into God's hands this time last year," said the farmer.

"And God's hands have delivered you back into mine," said Dan with a chuckle. Dan refused to seek out a woman for him until the £10 was paid and an extra £50 deposit on top of it. Perished as the farmer was, he had no choice. Finally when Dan had an account of a woman for him he demanded another £50. When the money was handed over Dan introduced him to the woman and left the fellow to his own devices.

He rarely pressed a client who reneged on him. If a man hadn't the decency to honour his bond Dan felt he was no longer worth bothering with. If Dan had been paid in full for all his endeavours there's no doubt he would have ended up a rich man.

Chapter 30

Although Dan's immense strength was not legendary during his lifetime he was, nevertheless, recognised as one of the strongest men in the country for his weight and height which was slightly under five feet ten inches. Chris Jer Davy Nolan, who presently farms in Renagown, remembers a great trial of Dan Paddy Andy's physical prowess in the year 1946.

"We were on our way to the big fair in Castleisland," Chris recalls, "my father Jer Davy, another man and myself, when one of the heifers we were driving slipped off the road and wound up in a dyke. She sank fast and very soon she was up to her neck in the muck and ooze. Lucky we had a rope and though we couldn't pull her out we managed to keep her head over. It took the three of us on the rope to stop her from sinking. We couldn't budge her an inch until Dan Paddy Andy came along.

"Let go the rope," he told us.

"Do whatever Dan tells ye," my father told us. "We let go the rope and Dan knelt down. He caught the heifer's two horns in his hands and started to pull. He didn't puff or pant or anything else but he pulled that heifer out without putting a strain on himself. We never saw anything like it."

"He was," said Dr Johnny Walsh, "probably the strongest man I ever encountered and pound for pound the best fist fighter I ever saw. He could have been another Jack La Motta if his talents had been exploited in time."

Dr Johnny was himself an Irish welterweight champion and was capped five times for the Leinster rugby team.

"Dan was a natural fighter," said Dr Johnny, "but what gave him that extra edge was his extraordinary strength."

Now and then there would be a minor fracas in the dance-hall. Dan's treatment for these outbreaks was simple and effective. First he would temporarily eject the miscreants. Secondly he would bang their heads together. This was his favourite method of chastisement. Rarely did he resort to his fists. On rare occasions when he would be called upon to defend himself from those who resented his authority he would spin his opponent round and round until he became dizzy when he would bring the gyrations to a halt and implant a well aimed kick on the scoundrel's posterior.

Once after ejecting a young gentleman, an experienced amateur boxer from the town of Tralee, Dan found himself at the receiving end of several unexpected and savage blows to the face. He almost lost consciousness but he managed to hold on when a few of his neighbours intervened. The boxer was shaping himself up for more and in language most foul declared that he would polish off Dan Paddy Andy for good and glory if he wasn't re-admitted to the hall. Dan's face, according to people who were present on the occasion, was a mass of blood and bruises.

"Let me go," Dan called to those of his friends who would shield him from further attack. Breaking loose he made straight for the boxer. The blows rained on him but he endured all until he got a chance to land a clout. One was all that was necessary. It landed on the Adam's apple. Six months would pass before the boxer returned to normality. Dan's authority was never seriously challenged after that.

According to Dan Canty, Dan Paddy Andy had a fatal weakness. He was a poor judge of horses. His lifelong love of horses was to prove too expensive a hobby and "although," as Tom Doran put it, "he was making coin on all fronts most of it was swept away by foolish investments in horses."

"The bother," said Tom "was that poor Dan couldn't see the horses right and when a horse was trotted out for inspection it was nearly always substituted by a kicker or a rogue before the sale."

"The trouble with me," said Dan himself in retrospect "was that I'd go by the form of the man that owned the horse instead of going by the form of the horse itself."

"They would have broken him in the end," said Dan Canty, "but for his son Paddy buying a Dodge pick-up."

Dan Paddy Andy was less dependent on the horse after that but he still loved to trade in horses. The consequences were not as disastrous, however, as they were in the pre-Dodge days.

"Dan Paddy Andy could live," said Dan Canty, "where another would starve and when he didn't get his way by action he got his way by grumbling. I remember saying to him once when he was giving out about the small fee he was offered by a strong farmer that there was no use in grumbling.

" 'True for you,' he said. 'There's no use in grumbling unless you're well able to grumble.' "

Chapter 31

If Dan were alive and thought that an account of his doings was being put together without special reference to the Smearla he would have cried halt! If you wanted to rile him all that needed to be done was to pass a single derogatory comment about the small, swift river of his birthplace.

"Blasht you," Dan would say, "what do you know about rivers?" More than once, Tom Doran recalled, he exhibited total amazement when clients from faraway places reluctantly acknowledged under questioning that they had never heard of the Smearla which was to Dan what the Tiber was to Caius Julius.

The valley of the Smearla is, without doubt, verdant and beautiful. Several miles long it is so narrow in places that it barely contains the delightful river from which it borrows its name. It abounds in sally groves and fraochan bushes, wild plum and crab trees with a bird population of thousands. Ouzels and dippers are here in plenty and the rare kingfisher hovers where the banks are high and the leafy cover deep. Snipe, pheasant, curlew and mallard abound in the rich cover along its many tiny tributaries.

It is also the source of several enduring songs but more important, for our narrative, it is the main watercourse for the Stacks and Glanruddery Mountains.

The Smearla is not a long river. It traverses a mere twenty-five miles before it joins the Feale but it is a unique river in that its waters are almost completely free from pollution and it never dries up as do most spate rivers. Dan Paddy Andy loved the Smearla and in his poaching days took many a sea trout and salmon from its numerous pools. He knew every song written about this most musical of streams. I first discovered he was a poet when I heard him talking about the Smearla. He never waxed less than eloquent and while he could be mundane about other things he chose his language with infinite care when dwelling upon his favourite river. Many's the threepenny bit I earned for singing his favourite song: "Close Down by the Sweet Smearla Side". It dwelt with the plight of a girl who was well-known to Dan:

> And now to conclude and to finish
> My sad and my mournful tale
> An advice I will give to all females
> Not to let their true loves under sail.
> For courted I was by a young man
> And the oceans do now us divide
> And he left me to wander in sorrow
> All alone by the sweet Smearla side.

To listen to Dan Paddy Andy tracing the course of the Smearla was to listen to pure music. He could never bear to be long away from its banks and I will always recall him sitting on a small elevation from which several hundred yards of its course could easily be followed, although not by Dan in his later years because of his restricted vision.

The Smearla was the chief reason he never emigrated to America or so he said.

"I could never leave it behind and there was no way I could take it with me." It is a most pleasant and songful stream as I know myself from fishing there in bygone days. "What would I do without the chatter and the singing of it?" Dan would say fondly when tracing its course.

Some years before he died I taped a talk of his which dealt with the names of the townlands through which it passed.

"She starts her gallop," said Dan, "out of a small well in Knockadariffe away back there in the mountain. To tell the Gospel truth and not to wrong either side she divides the townlands of Knockadariffe and Bruachán. There's a song called 'Sweet Bruachán' but if you were to unite Ireland this minute I couldn't remember a line of it. She takes her time then, which isn't natural to her, until she takes off with the fall of ground once more and lands herself here beside us in Renagown. I think Renagown would be the place she loves the best. It would be. It would be. Across from us at the other side is Dromadamore. She keeps the two apart."

Here is the countryside of the immortal Thade Gowran whose songs "The Yorkshire Pigs" and "The High-Heeled Shoes" are still firm favourites among the people. But let us return to Dan Paddy Andy as he continues to describe the Smearla's downward journey from the mountain.

"After Renagown," Dan went on, "she stops her dawdling and proceeds like a greyhound between Carrigcannon and Dromadabeg. She's white here and she's noisy here and you wouldn't want to take her on in a flood. Any salmon that comes this far comes on a one-way ticket," Dan went on.

"She races then as if the devil was after her apast the lovely church of Lyreacrompane. This is serviced by the priests down below in the parish of Duagh. A great place for priests Duagh. More priests came out of Duagh than came out of Rome. Every second gorsoon there was turned into a priest. There's a fine stand of spruce here and greenery galore between the chapel and the river and I declare to God there must be more birds here than anywhere else in the country. This place is green in the height of winter and no matter how black or bitter the weather there is always some make of a bird sure to be singing." Here Dan might pause and address himself to the sky.

"Where is she now?" he would say, taking off his hat and scratching his head. "I'll tell you where she is now. She's after passing the creamery of Lyreacrompane without a salute or a beck the same as if it wasn't there at all. From there she dances through Glashnanoon and Knockanebrack and finally faldaddles her way where she shakes hands with the Feale at the joinings of Inchamagillery which lies between Ballinruddery and Trieneragh."

One could sense the affection he bore this delightful little river from the way he spoke about it.

"The Smearla," said Dan, "is short and sweet like an ass's gallop."

One of the best of the Smearla poets is a man called P.J. Brosnan. He was a friend of Dan's. He is still alive in West Limerick and hale and hearty to boot. It was he who composed "Down by the Smearla Side" another favourite of Dan's:

> To our exiles who have crossed the sea,
> We send this wish to you:

We hope you always will remain
To God and Ireland true.
It is our earnest prayer today
That your footsteps He may guide
And bring you safely home again
To the lovely Smearla side.

Possibly it's a song which might have little significance for city dwellers who never felt the full impact of emigration the way country people did. The former were merely changing one urban scene for another. For Dan the song had a special meaning. His sons and daughter, through no fault of their own or of Dan's, were compelled to take the emigrant ship for the want of employment at home. There was and is little likelihood that they will ever return to the banks of the Smearla.

Chapter 32

One evening outside his famous dancehall in Renagown as the sun was setting behind the high hill of Carrigcannon Dan Paddy Andy was passing the time, exchanging news snippets with some other elders of the neighbourhood when somebody suddenly sang the praises of the fine weather which was part of a heat wave brightening the country at the time.

"M'anam ón diabhal," observed the lover of the fine days, "is there anything to beat settled weather. It cheers both man and bashte and there's no shortage of growth or anything."

"I don't know," said Dan. "Fine weather is alright but it won't do away with work. Won't you have to save the hay and won't you have to cock it?" Here he paused and polished his spectacles to allow himself time for the framing of his next observation. He went on, "Won't you have to turn the turf? Won't you have to make it into stoolins and horse stoolins and knock it again if it don't dry?

"Won't you have to draw it out of the bog and won't you have to make a reek of it and won't you have to cut rushes for to thatch the reek?" There were murmurs of agreement.

"It appears to me," he concluded philosophically, "that there is a deal more money to be made at the shady side of a hedge of a wet day working the head."

The meaning of this declaration did not escape his more astute listeners. What Dan implied was that a wet day made work impossible but while waiting for the rain to pass a man might profitably plan new undertakings while he stood or sat in the shade. Indeed this was the story of Dan's life and when he approved of novel undertakings he was simply vindicating the course his own multifarious career had taken.

Now there happened to be in the company at the time a cranky sort of man who could let nothing pass without putting a damper on it. He was forever casting dark shadows on the bright side of things.

"He favours the single way of life," said Dan of him once, "for he can make no fist of a woman and how could he and he given so much to cnawvshawling and cronawning. Seldom

136

indeed will you hear the good word out of the hoor."

"Dang you," said Dan to him. "Here you are with your meadows cut and cocked and your corn ripening and all that's left to do now is milk your cows and let the dry days do the rest."

"Wet day or dry day," said the aingisheoir in his lonesome way, "there is a widow in the townland of Tubbersharrive what won't have nothing to do with me, what won't return my salutes and what will dive like a duck through the handiest hedge when we meet on the road."

His tone was such it seemed that Dan Paddy Andy was to blame for the widow's indifference. This was far from being the case, however, for Dan had several times spoken to the widow in question on the fellow's behalf. All to no avail however. She complained that he had black teeth and lonesome ways but even these she was prepared to overlook if he made some attempt to indicate what precisely he had in store for her. Dan listened carefully to all the cranky man had to say but after a while it dawned on him that unless he intervened there would be no end to the fellow's complaining.

"Blasht you!" said Dan impatiently, "wouldn't you make a drive at her and take her in your arms and swear your honest love for her and hould her for a minute by the butt of the ear with them two black fangs o' yours. A kettle was never boiled without fire and a woman was never won by wishing." Having said this Dan Paddy Andy cast a contemptuous look in the direction of the whiner and announced finally that corn cannot be cut without edge.

It was plain talk but it worked. Our man must have taken the bull by the horns for he was legally married to the widow in the fall of that same year and whether they lived happily ever after is something that only they themselves can tell you for they gave no sign, one way or the other, to the public in general as to whether they were content or not. There can be no doubt but that the marriage was perfected for issue appeared within the prescribed time.

Again Dan Paddy Andy was the loser for what did our once-cranky friend declare but that Dan had played no active part in securing the wife; that all he did was offer some advice as a matter of course; that he was, therefore, entitled to no payment save maybe a glass of porter out of the goodness of the cranky man's heart should they meet sometime in a public house.

When he directed himself towards philosophy, Dan Paddy Andy was at his most revealing and amusing. Once he got going on this tack you could shoot him any kind of a question and be certain of a worthwhile answer.

"What do you think of love at first sight, Dan?"

"Would you buy a mare by the looks of her or would you trot her first? Would you boil a spud before buying a butt?"

"So what do you think of sex, Dan?"

"Sex is fine, as long as it don't go to the head."

I doubt if Dan ever heard the expression "city slickers" but when advising young girls at their first dances he must have had these same slickers in mind.

"Most townies are alright but never give your heart to the buck with the hair oil, the tie pin and the fountain pen or the man with the swanky talk because that's the very man that will give you the crack of a fist if you don't have something in the pan for him when the pubs close at night."

"What about drink, Dan?"

"M'anam ón diabhal, there's nothing wrong with drink unless you make it your diet." He was full of parables about the evils of drink.

"There was a cousin of mine," said Dan, "went one time to Killarney to see Danno Mahony wrestling Charlie Strick in the racecourse there. That would be 1933, the year after the Eucharistic Congress. I had my sight in them days boy. Didn't this cousin fall to drinking whiskey and didn't he hold at it hard for three days. The night of the third day he was carried into the mental home. He was roaring like Horan's bull and he made out to the Civic Guards that he was after being attacked by wild deer that came down from the mountains in the middle of the night. When he scolded the deer they changed themselves into greyhounds. Of course they were greyhounds all the time but that's three days of whiskey for you. He gave six months indoors in Killarney and he stuck to mediums of porter after he was released."

Dan was extremely witty but the one thing he did not possess was a sharp tongue. When the Renagown hall was going strong there was a well-known Tralee band which went under the name of Locke, Herrity and Hayes. Dan never succeeded in enticing this fine combo to Renagown but when Locke got a job as a porter in a bank in Tralee at a time when it was impossible to get a job of any kind Dan was delighted with Locke's good fortune.

"I'm not one bit surprised," said Dan. "A bank without a Locke in the door is no bank."

In the early Forties in the district of North Kerry a well-constructed, handsome farmer's son played havoc with the hearts of the more innocent serving girls who were taken in by his guile. The result was at least four pregnancies and, more probable than not, as many more concealed by one means or another. It was said that this Lothario had gone within twelve months of being ordained for the priesthood and that his pious manner coupled with his religious blandishments had the effect of disarming unwary females of all ages. Rumour had it that he intended paying a visit to Dan Paddy Andy's hall at the Cross of Renagown. To forestall this unwelcome prospect Dan stood on a chair one night and made one of his rare but memorable announcements:

"I say to ye," said Dan, "that if the ram of God comes this way he'll go home a wether."

As Dan's fortunes took an upward swing he was often the target of uncharitable remarks. The worst of these was in the shape of a satire written by a local poetaster. He was a tall, thin, reedy sort of a fellow who had a very high opinion of himself as a poet. One night in the Three Elms, Al Roche's famous hostelry in Lyreacrompane, Dan was asked what he thought of this man as a composer of poems.

"All I'll say," said Dan, "is that he hasn't the arse of a poet. To be a poet," Dan went on, "you need a big, soft, wide bottom to be sitting down on and this poor aingisheoir, God pity him, has a behind like a brace of duckeggs in a handkerchief."

"But what has a man's behind to do with poetry?" asked a listener.

Dan said nothing for a while. The talk of the time was all about the installation of three reconditioned long-range guns which had been installed at Portshannon, north of Ballylongford. These were to remain part of our coastal defences for the duration of the Emergency until 1945. Thousands of tons of concrete went into their bases and whenever there was artillery practice the windows rattled in the village of Bally-longford several miles away. Dan had all this in mind as he considered his answer.

"I'll tell you," said Dan, "a poet needs a big bottom if he is to fire broadsides that will knock walls. Without an arse all he'll fire is spits and venom."

A deep murmur of approval went round the gathering. As usual Dan Paddy Andy had weighed his words well before making his pronouncement. The sager among those present were agreed about one thing. It was a foolish man who took potshots at Dan Paddy Andy because when he returned fire there was no place to hide.

Chapter 33

"I went over the Ivy Bridge as grey as a goat and as ould as a bush, but I came out of there a boy, and if the woman Dan promised me wasn't all he said she was, she was as good as could be expected and she done me fine. I didn't draw a sober breath till I had recourse to that woman. I was a rake and a good-for-nothing. I tell you I had a like to throw myself over that bridge to drown myself but I felt like a swim after I seeing Dan. I gave him £2 in earnest money and he said to me, 'Go home now, whitewash the house, keep away from the bottle and I'll be making out a woman for you.'"

Many a man like the self-admitted rake who left the foregoing testament had the same story to tell. With the opposite sex it was different. They would usually contact Dan by letter or through an intermediary. It just wouldn't do if they were seen calling to Dan's abode in Renagown. Instead Dan called to them and there would be long sessions involving the girl herself and her parents in the Room. According to Paddy Doran these interviews could go on for hours. Dan was most meticulous. He had to have all the facts and figures for later when he would be making the girl's case he would be interviewed himself. All sorts of questions would be asked and if satisfactory answers were not forthcoming the girl's chances could well be ruined.

Lyreacrompane is not and was never an easy place to find. Modern-day commercial travellers and government officials have frequently failed to locate it. From Lyre one must pass through Carrigcannon before descending to the Ivy Bridge which is the gateway to Renagown. In Dan's heyday travellers from the northern side who sought him out were obliged to take this route. There are many splendid views along this itinerary. From the top of Carrig Hill one can see the course of the Smearla, all of Renagown and several of the surrounding townlands. As one descends Carrig there is a narrow road which branches off at the right and which passes through great, wild groves and vast state forests before joining the Tralee Road three miles from the town's racecourse. This is easily the most scenic road in North Kerry and although extremely narrow it is always passable. The Glaise Riabhach also accompanies the traveller on his way for several miles. Dan Paddy Andy used to say that there was gold in the streams in this part of the world if one was willing to search. Before one makes the steep descent to Tralee there is a beautiful view of Tralee Bay and, of course, the town itself.

Of all the small bridges that span small rivers or streams none has the romantic image created by the Ivy Bridge. I crossed it for the first time in my life in the summer of 1936 and must have crossed it back and forth, drunk and sober, 500 times since. For me it has always remained a symbol of division and in another sense transition. It divides my world in two, the real and the romantic. Once over the bridge I am in Tír na nÓg once more and when I first crossed it in Dan Paddy Andy's heyday I swapped the town for the country for the first time. In the end I find myself half-town, half-country, thanks to the magic world which lies beyond Ivy Bridge, the land of Dan Paddy Andy.

This one-eyed, ivy covered structure spans the Glashouriogh or Glaise Riabhach, which simply means the speckled stream because its course is mottled with white, brown and black boulders when the water is low. It is the largest of the Smearla tributaries. A hundred yards away is the Sheehy house where I used to holiday during the summers of the late Thirties and early Forties.

In the winter of 1976 the bridge was closed for repairs, causing great upset to the milk-producing farmers in the Lyreacrompane hinterland; but it was only a temporary set-back and it was opened again in March of the following year. The end result is that large creamery lorries can now cross the bridge which was hitherto too narrow.

In the Thirties and Forties before the motor car was to become commonplace, the Ivy Bridge was a significant landmark in the topography of North Kerry. Anybody from north of Renagown who wished to visit Dan was obliged to cross this bridge.

It was also a popular trysting place and if a man from outside the area was courting a lady from Renagown or beyond the bridge was the obvious place to rendezvous. On occassional fine days near the end of his time above ground Dan would saunter down from Renagown Cross and take up his position at the bridge. He did this purely for company's sake. No sooner would he have himself seated on the low parapet than a passing car would stop and its occupants bid him the time of day. His name was a household word around this time.

During my childhood the bridge was the local forum and many is the deep debate which was conducted there. There was at the time working in the locality an Irish teacher by the name of Seán Kavanagh. He hailed from the Dingle Gaeltacht and he greatly enriched my knowledge of the local scene. With loving care and diligence he would explain the meaning of the names of Glounamucmae, Carrigcannon, Muingaminnane, Tooreensharrive, Dormadamore, Dromadabeg, Tooreenastooka, Knockatarrive and so on. He was one of the best teachers of Irish I ever knew. For instance until Seán came we believed that the English for Glounamucmae was the Glen of the Fat Pigs whereas its true meaning is The Glen of the Plentiful Plain.

At that time there were hundreds of Irish words and phrases alive in the language of the people of the Stacks and rarely did Dan Paddy Andy use a sentence which was not flavoured with Irish. He was, of course, quite unaware of this. For a chap of my years and literary leanings Seán Kavanagh was heaven-sent. The best part was that I never realised I was being taught. Rather did I lap up the precious knowledge he let fall. This was his greatness. My sons were very lucky too to have him for a friend and teacher in later years in the Irish College in Ballybunion. Seán married lovely Kit McElligott of Dromadamore, one of the same McElligotts who specialised in the manufacture of the home-made butter. They still live happily, in retirement, in that same Gaeltacht where Seán first saw the light of day.

But back to Dan Paddy Andy lest his ghost haunt me for not fulfilling my main contract. One summer's evening a crowd of us youngsters made our way from Jer Davy's inch, where we had been kicking football, to the Ivy Bridge. There were a number of men gathered there. A short time before two German mechanics who operated a huge turf-cutting machine in the great bog of Lyreacrompane proper had been interned in the Curragh and there was much speculation as to whether they would try to escape and return to Lyreacrompane. There was also at the time much talk of spies and invasions and any unfortunate stranger who came the way was closely inspected by man, woman and child. Not many commercial travellers came to Lyre and Renagown but when one did he was vetted from head to toe.

On that particular evening I had a few pence in my pocket so we made our way from the bridge up Carrig Hill to Nolan's shop where it was still possible to invest in a packet of Woodbines and have a surreptitious smoke.

As we made our way to the brow of Carrig a mare and trap appeared suddenly in front of us. The driver was a large, stout, elderly man; a grey-haired, prosperous looking fellow, well-dressed with a gold chain across his portly belly. He was the kind of man who commanded instant respect. When he drew rein we stopped still and stared at him. When he addressed us he did so in the haughtiest way imaginable.

"Tell me," said he, "where would I find the abode of Dan Paddy Andy O'Sullivan?"

We explained that Dan was presently at the bottom of the hill, seated on the bridge. The man alighted from the trap after he had weighed off the gradient of the hill. He decided to lead the animal downwards while we followed behind out of pure curiosity. At the bridge the conversation stopped the moment the stranger arrived there. No word was spoken for a while. He could well be one of Dan's natural enemies in disguise, to wit, a blind pensions' officer or he might be a spy although the latter was extremely unlikely. He looked every inch a farmer which was what he turned out to be.

"Tell me," he said after a while, "which of you is Dan Paddy Andy?"

"Which of you is Dan Paddy Andy?" Dan himself asked in order to divert attention. There was no answer forthcoming.

"What's he wanted for?" asked Martin Sheehy, the head of the household of which I was part.

"It's private," the short answer came back.

"Sing dumb if you like," said Martin Sheehy, "but state your case or be gone. Now what do you want Dan for?"

"I want him to make out a woman for me," said the visitor without batting an eyelid. Only then did Dan step forward.

"I'm the man you want," he said. "Untackle your mare at the next gate and let her graze the long acre."

"No need for the long acre," said he. "She'll have her fill of oats for I'm a man that never neglects a mare or a female."

So saying he led the animal to the gate and proceeded to tie a bag of oats over her head. While he was out of earshot the conversation started again.

"What does an oul' buck like that want a woman for?" asked the local cnawvshawler or whiner, the man for whom Dan had provided a wife and who was never happy unless he was complaining about something.

"'Tis an old cock won't pick oats," Dan answered, "as you well know for you were no cockerel yourself."

"That may be," said the whiner, "but 'tis an unnatural thing all the same to see an oul pensioner looking for female company. What sort of a world would we have at all if our fathers and grandfathers took to the roads after women? Who'd be there to keep an eye to the child or scold the cat?"

"Listen," said Dan losing his temper. "If you saw two asses coupling, would you question the age of the jackass or would you deny him his share of the natural joys of the world; or if you saw a pair of crows threading, would you ask the cock for a birth certificate? You would not," said Dan, "but you'd condemn a Christian. 'Tis alright for asses and crows but not for the likes of that poor man there."

The cnawvshawler had no argument against this defence so he tried another tack.

"What could he do," he asked, "for a young lady with taspy on her?"

"He never said he wanted a young lady," said Dan.

"He wouldn't turn his back on one," said the whiner.

"The older the fiddle," said Dan, "the sweeter the tune."

What a great attorney Dan would have made. I never remember him to have been beaten in an argument.

"What about his white hair?" asked the whiner finally.

"A cabbage," said Dan, "is no use till it's white."

Like many a man before him the cnawvshawler wished he had never opened his mouth. It would take Daniel O'Connell himself to match Dan Paddy Andy when it came to exchanging words.

It transpired that the man in the trap wanted a woman in the forties, someone settled to take the place of his mother who had just passed over to the other side at the age of ninety. When Dan explained that his charge would be a pound note per cow the man tried to knock him down to 10s. When Dan held firm he asked him to take 15s. for each cow. Dan still held firm. It transpired that this man had sixty milch cows and that was his reason for trying to get a reduction in the price. Dan eventually fixed him up with a wife. She was one of his own kind, the sister of a well-to-do farmer from beyond Tralee. Dan always maintained that land married land. On this occasion he was right.

He had extreme difficulty in collecting his fee. The more money people have the less likely they are to part with it. In the end after consistent endeavour failed to win him justice Dan was obliged to resort to epistolary threats. The last thing he wanted to to was to go into court. Eventually, rather than end up empty-handed, he would settle for half the money.

One of Dan's favourite stories about the law concerned two Listowel solicitors. Two brothers from the Stacks Mountains had a bitter fight. Both were convinced that the other was wrong so they went to Listowel to see the family solicitor. It was a case of first come first served. The brother who called secondly was told by the solicitor in question that he had been retained by the brother and, on that account, could not act for him.

"However," said he, "I'll give you a note to a colleague of mine and he'll look after you."

Duly he gave him the note. It was in a sealed envelope. Our friend, out of curiosity, decided to have a look inside as soon as he left the solicitor's office. The note was terse.

"Dear George," it read, "here is a fine fat goose for you. Pluck him well and I'll pluck his brother."

Dan was often obliged to resort to the law in order to collect his fees. "And when you're done with the law," said Dan, "it's aisy count what's left."

Dan was greviously wronged by the law but his friends, who still abound in Renagown and Lyre, have suggested that it would do more harm than good to resurrect that tragic miscarriage of justice here. They insist, however, that Dan Dan was never the same afterwards.

"I remember too," Chris Jer Davy told me, "when accounts came from England that two fine young men, as fine as ever drew breath, were after dying Dan broke down completely although they were not related to him. They used to dance in the hall you see before they went to England, and God they were fine fellows, great workers. Coalmining they were in Leicester but it got them after a few years. The dust stuck to the lungs and finished them off in their prime. Dan was heartbroken. He closed the hall for a time. They were two lads that always behaved themselves. They were Michael O'Connell from Carrigcannon and Denis Reidy from Cunnaceen."

I knew Michael O'Connell. We played football together along Jer Davy's inches during my summers in Renagown. He was a natural athlete, God be good to him.

"Don't ever go mining," Dan warned Chris Nolan and a group of other youths after the passing of the young men. "It's not natural to go under the ground before your time. Soon enough we'll have to go under forever."

The loss of his sons, the deaths of Michael O'Connell and Dinny Reidy, the murder of Maurice Moore and the unjust treatment by the law were blows which nearly devastated Dan Paddy Andy.

"Dan was soft at heart," Paddy Doran recalls. "He felt for others. All he ever wanted was to pull up the man with nothing. Of course, he had no mercy for the man with money. He was a kind of a Robin Hood that way."

Paddy Doran well remembers Dan's uncontrollable anger when well-made men of wealth and substance would scoff and laugh when it became known that Dan was match-making for some desperate pauper or for some unfortunate person with a deformity.

"I saw him catch a big, important fellow by the throat in a pub," said Paddy, "and shake him and say, 'Everyman is entitled to a woman, you begrudging thief you.' That was the kind Dan was," Paddy concluded. "He wanted fair play for the man at the bottom as well as the man at the top."

Chapter 34

Dan Paddy Andy O'Sullivan, great matchmaker and human being, drew the last of all his breaths of a bitter March evening in the Year of Our Lord 1966. Nobody seems to be certain about the exact date of his birth but it is believed he was born in the year 1900 in Renagown.

On the day he died the Smearla was in fine fettle with a banker of a flood which swept all impurities before it in readiness for the first of the spring salmon which waited far downriver in the Cashen estuary for the brown floodwaters to subside.

Dan would have enjoyed the Smearla on such a day, the swirling pools under the sallies, the rich chuckling where the eddies were deepest, the white-crested tumult where its passage was roughest over black boulders old as time and the hundred other cadences high and low which all amount to beautifully orchestrated music when a man has an ear for river water.

Dan was possessed of this ear. Joe Sheehy recalls that Dan would spend the best part of a day listening to the Glaise Riabhach. "If the water was high he'd lean over the parapet and listen," Joe recalls. "After a while he'd go to the other side and listen there too."

His obsession with the Smearla may well have arisen from the fact that he was never able to fully discern the delicate colours and shapes of the Stacks Mountains in his final years. He, therefore, turned from the visual aspect of his environment to seek compensation in the songs and other sounds of the Smearla.

Dan died from heart failure. It had followed him in his declining years, restricted his movements to the houses of his immediate neighbours and confined him for the most part to his own hearth. He died peacefully and without any evidence of great pain although he was also plagued by stomach cancer. Still it was the heart that finished him. For several years before his death he was in the habit of rambling to Martin Sweeney's house which was only a short walk from his own abode. His wife Kate would accompany him part of the way and one of the Sweeneys would always walk back with him.

The Sweeneys loved his visits. He was a great storyteller and they would sit enraptured while he told and retold the tales which had made him a living legend. Always these stories would be coloured by whimsy and humour. That same humour of Dan's still remains in Renagown. It is part and parcel of every story and every exchange of words. It is to be found alive and well and kicking in the Four Elms pub in Carrigcannon. It is to be found in the folk plays of George Fitzmaurice and the ballads of Thade Gowran whose "Yorkshire Pigs" is still a firm favourite wherever ballads are sung:

> Up and down aroon from Glashnanoon
> And from Brosna to Meengwee,
> There'll be slips and stores from well-bred boars
> To supply the whole countree.
> If the cratur stays small he'll make tay for them all,
> Currant bread made from raisins and figs,
> And the creameries soon will pay cheques in the moon
> For to fatten the Yorkshire Pigs.

Martin Sweeney's brother Peter, now in America, was Dan's personal barber. He was once filling in an employment form when he came to the question of his trade or profession, if any. He was tempted to write "Barber to His Excellency Dan Paddy Andy O'Sullivan, Chief of Renagown" but he changed his mind for it was more than likely that the prospective employers might not see the humour. On the other hand a time could well be at hand when such a credential might very nearly be priceless.

Peter Sweeney would shave Dan regularly and on rare occasions he would give him a haircut. Dan retained a fine head of curls to the very end and when people would remark upon this Dan would always say, "Them are the same curls that brought Kate O'Brien off her perch."

It was Kate who found him dead. She had been in the haggard counting the hens. She found him lying on his bed with a look of peace and contentment on his face. Shortly afterwards young Mary Hickey, daughter of the same Mickey and Noranne matched by Dan in 1939, happened to call by chance. She was dispatched at once for her father. Mickey Hickey and Martin Sweeney came at once. Then came Patey Cremins and Connie Brosnan from Dromadabeg. The four between them washed and shaved Dan and laid him out in his best suit. A messenger was sent to the presbytery in Clogher. Then the litany was recited and before they rose from their knees Father Murphy was on the scene.

It was time now for other matters. Martin Sweeney was dispatched to Al Roche's pub, two miles away, to order drink for the wake. Then America would have to be contacted and Dan's sons and daughter notified. This would be done by Neelus Nolan of Lyreacrompane post office. There were others who had to be notified, friends and relations all over the countryside.

Recently I asked Martin Sweeney if he heard or saw anything unusual on the night Dan died.

"I did," said Martin. "I heard fierce pillalloing over Jereen Davy's inch and what cocks there were in Lyre crew till the stroke of twelve." Many others in Renagown heard similar cries coming from the same direction.

"It wasn't a dog and it wasn't human," Tom Doran recalls. "It could only have been the banshee."

There were other happenings of significance. A light was seen in Kilbanavan graveyard in Castleisland around the time Dan gave up the ghost. Martin Sweeney's car refused to start, a thing that never happened before.

Further up from Renagown, in the house of Din Joe Mahony of Muingaminnane, the cocks crowed in unison on the stroke of eight, precisely the time Dan gave over life. By Din Joe's own testimony, a clock that had been going without failure for seventy-two years stopped and never went again. On a more humourous note, a black cat owned by the Mahonys ran under a bed and could not be coaxed out until it came of its own accord two days later.

In Carrigcannon, according to Joe Sheehy of Renagown, lights were seen around two houses and stayed shining till cockcrow. On the parapet of the Ivy Bridge in Renagown another light was seen. There were other happenings and from these accounts it will be gathered that the gentle humour of Dan Paddy Andy had not gone into the grave with him.

He was waked well and his children came to bury him. He was churched in Clogher but it was in Kilbanavan in Castleisland that he chose to be buried.

He had made this clear long before he died and it wasn't such a black day after all when they lowered him into the grave where lay the mortal remains of the two young sons he loved so dearly. In a niche in the East Wall of Kilbanavan there is a small cross erected to his memory and to the memory of his sons.

As I write this, seventeen years after his death, one certainty begins to emerge and that is that there will be many books written about Dan Paddy Andy. I hear that researchers are circulating around Lyreacrompane and more power to them. They will find their tasks to be enormously rewarding, and if there will be outrageous stories attributed to Dan in the future it is well to remember that all great men have attracted the same kind of attention when they were safely under the clay. Dan has been credited with a thousand statements ranging from the sublime to the ridiculous, but it is certain that he never uttered a quarter of them.

It would be a work of the greatest importance if somebody or some group were to record the 400 marriages for which Dan was responsible and to determine, as far as is possible, how the marriages worked out. The one failure, which he never denied, was not Dan's fault, although he would always insist that it was or, at least, he was willing to share the responsibility for the failure. To list the 399 other marriages against the social background of the period and to draw accurate conclusions would greatly benefit modern society. It would be the most important sociological work ever undertaken in that vast area where Dan was sole matchmaker for the best part of his life.

My own memory of Dan is an abiding one. We got on famously together from the first moment we met. I still see him plainly sitting on a small rock overlooking the Smearla, leaning forward on his stout stick or standing hopefully on Sunday nights outside the hall in Renagown endeavouring to whip up business.

"Come on in boys. Plenty cotton here."

All the cotton, alas, was to go and when the girls go the

boys are sure to follow. Over the course of Dan's lifetime more than half the houses and holdings in his neighbourhood were to disappear altogether from the scene. He did his utmost to halt this devastating decline but the odds were stacked too highly against him. Still let it stand to his credit that he never threw in the towel.

Today from Renagown and Lyreacrompane there are twelve travelling to work at the Kerry Co-op complex in Listowel and many more travelling to factories in Tralee and Killarney.

There was no factory in Dan's time and so the boys and girls had to leave forever, but Dan kept faith with the future and it looks now that Renagown might once again be able to maintain a small dancehall if the people so wished.

Not long before he died Dan was one day conversing with John Moloney of Dromadamore.

"I'll never forget the way he spoke on that occasion," John recalls. "It was as if he was telling me we would not see each other again."

"I am the last of the Andys here," Dan said. "My seed is scattered wide and doing well but this is my place and this is where I want to make my goodbyes to the memory of my father and his father. I have left my stamp upon this place and upon these people and when I'm gone, as sure as there's a snipe in Raemore, there will be talk of Dan Paddy Andy and his doings from time to time."

> As I walked out through the land of Lyre
> The beaded dews did the fields attire
> And the old grey world was turned to fire
> In the month of May in the morning.
> Out of the bowers by the bright rays lit
> Lark and linnet and long-tailed tit
> And every other that ever did flit
> Sang loud of the sun's adorning.
>
> Sang from the foliage green and gay,
> Sang for the sake of the new-born day,
> Sang for the blossoming loves of May
> And sang for the rude and the randy.

Sang for a soul too long reproved,
Sang for a soul that was never loved
As over the Ivy Bridge he roved
To the land of Dan Paddy Andy.

Appendix 1

Placenames and their Meanings

Ballincollig
Baile an Chullaigh: the townland of the boar.

Ballinruddery
Baile an Riodaraigh: Riddle's townland. Also there is some local belief that it may be Baile an Ridire, The townland of the knight.

Ballybunion
Baile an Bhuinneánaigh: The townland of O'Bunnions or O'Bannions.

Ballyheigue
Baile ui Theidg: O'Teigue's townland.

Ballylongford
Béal Átha Longphuirt: The ford-mouth of the fortress (Carrigafoyle Castle).

Beenageeha
Binn na gaoithe: The windy peak or summit.

Broughane
Bruachán: Border, fringe or boundary.

Carntoohill
Corrán Tuathail: Tuathal's Carn — Ireland's highest peak.

Carrigcannon
Carraig ceannfhionn: the white-tipped rock.

Cashen
Casán (Chiarraidhe): The pathway (of Kerry).

Cearcar
Carcair: A prison or rock cell.

Clogher
Clochar: The stony place

Cloughboola
Cloch Buaile: A stone-built shelter for cattle during the summer grazing season.

Cordal
Cordal / Cor Dá Ghleann: Two valleys coming together into a knot resembling a bow tie.

Cunnaceen
Cnocín: The little hill.

Duagh
Dubh Áth: The black ford — called after a ford on the River Feale when its course was below Duagh graveyard.

Dromadabeg
Droma fada beag: The low, long ridge.

Dromadamore
Drom fada mór: The high, long ridge.

Fahaduv
Faithche dubh: The black, open space.

Glanrudderies
Gleann ridire or rudaire: The glen of the knight. There is also a hill known as Knight's Mountain in the Glan-rudderies.

Glashnanoon
Glaise na n-uan: The stream of the lambs.

Glashouriogh
Glaise Riabhach: The speckled stream, so-called because the course of this stream is strewn with boulders and rocky outcrops.

Gleanndearg
Gleann dearg: The red glen.

Inchamagillery (also Inchamagilleragh)
Inse mhic Ghiolla Riabhaigh:The inch or water-meadow of McGilreavy.

Kilbanavan
Cill banbhán: The wood of the piglet.

Kilconlea
Cill con liath: The wood of the grey hound.

Killarney
Cill Áirne: The church of the sloe trees.

Knockaclare
Cnoc an Chláir: The hill of the slab or tablet.

Knockadirreen
Cnoc an Doirín: The hill of the oak grove.

Knockanebrack
Cnocán Breac: The speckled hill.

Knockatarrive (also Knockadarriffe)
Cnoc an tairbh: The hill of the bull.

Knocknagoshel
   Cnoc na gCaiseal: The hill of the oratories.
Listowel
   Lios Tuathail: The fort of Tuathal.
Lixnaw
   Lic Snámha: The flagstone of the swimming (Brick River).
Lyreacrompane
   Ladhar a'crompán: Ladhar is the land enclosed by two converging rivers or streams or by high, converging ridges. Crompán is a dry hillock surrounded in whole or part by marshy land.
Muingwee
   Muine Bhuí: The yellow, sedgy marsh.
Muingaminnane
   Muine a'mhionnáin: The sedgy marsh of the jacksnipe.
Rathea
   Ráth Íodha: The fort of the yew tree.
Raemore
   Ré mór: Ré is a stretch of ground. Mór is large.
Renagown
   Ré na ngamhan: The level ground of the calves.
Scartaglin
   Scartach an ghleanna or ghlaine: The (whitethorn) thicket of the glen.
Tanavalla
   (Garraí) an tseana-bhaile: The garden of the old townland or township.
Tooreenastooka
   Tuairín na stuaca: The green or bleaching place of the heights.
Toureenmore
   Tuairín mór: The big bleaching place or green.
Tournageehy
   Tuar na gaoithe: The windy lea or fallow.
Trieneragh
   Trían íarach: The western third — In medieval times a trían was the equivalent of four townlands.
Tubbernanoon
   Tobar na n-uan: The well of the lambs.

Appendix 2

Irish Words

Agusheen
    Aguisín: An addition.
Aingisheoir
    Ainniseoir: A miserable, penurious creature.
Amadán
    Amadán: Fool.
Bodhrawn
    Bodhrán: Skin drum.
Bogadawn
    Bogadán: A soft, unsteady person.
Cadhrawn
    Cadhrán: A small sod of turf or part of a sod.
Ciotóg
    Ciotóg: A left-handed person.
Cnawvshawling
    Cnáimhseáil: Act of complaining or grumbling.
Cronawning
    Crónán: Continuous humming or buzzing sound.
Dúchas: Birthright, heritage.
Fostook
    Fostúch: Boy of employable age.
Gallus
    Gealas: Brace(s).
Iochtar: Extra bonham in the litter for which the sow has no
    teat. Pet bonham.
M'anam ón diabhal: My soul from the devil.
Mawcal
    Máchail: Blemish.
Óinseach: A foolish, giddy woman.
Pillaloing
    Fuilibiliú: Hullabaloo, yell.
Shaughrawn
    Seachrán: Wandering, straying.

Sugawn
   Súgán: A hay or straw rope. In this instance a chair with a
   seat made from sugawns.
Tamall
   Tamall: Space of time, while.
Taspy
   Teaspach: Spirit, energy.
Tuathalach
   Tuathalach: Awkward.